Y0-BRP-015

Implementing the Learning Society

NEW STRATEGIES
FOR FINANCING
SOCIAL OBJECTIVES

Charles S. Benson

Harold L. Hodgkinson

with the assistance of
Jessica S. Pers

IMPLEMENTING
THE LEARNING
SOCIETY

Jossey-Bass Publishers

San Francisco · Washington · London · 1974

IMPLEMENTING THE LEARNING SOCIETY
New Strategies for Financing Social Objectives
by Charles S. Benson and Harold L. Hodgkinson

Copyright © 1974 by: Jossey-Bass, Inc., Publishers
615 Montgomery Street
San Francisco, California 94111
&
Jossey-Bass Limited
3 Henrietta Street
London WC2E 8LU

Library of Congress Catalogue Card Number LC 73-21072

International Standard Book Number ISBN 0-87589-220-5

Manufactured in the United States of America

JACKET DESIGN BY WILLI BAUM

FIRST EDITION

Code 7410

The
Jossey-Bass Series
in Higher Education

Preface

Implementing the Learning Society explores how the efficiency of colleges and universities can be enhanced. We believe that readers should be concerned about this topic for at least three reasons: the economic magnitude of higher education, the importance of the social benefits of higher education, and considerations of equity in providing higher education.

When an activity consumes a large amount of resources—either in the form of human skills, such as those of faculty members and administrative staff, or in the form of valuable buildings, laboratories, and supplies—that activity has social importance. The economic magnitude of higher education reveals its priority in our society. In 1970-1971, total expenditures in higher education were $23.5 billion ($14.9 billion in public institutions and $8.6 billion in private institutions), equaling 2.4 percent of our national product and representing a per capita cost of $113. Not an inconsequential sum! Furthermore, the rate of growth in expenditures for higher education has been astounding. Measured in 1970-1971 dollars, expenditures rose in the ten years from 1960-1961 to 1970-1971 from $8 billion to $23.5 billion. The annual rate of increase in higher education was 11.7 percent, while the per capita rate of increase in national product was only 2.7 percent. Thus, resource commitments to higher education have considerably outstripped growth in the capacity to support colleges and universities. It is estimated that by 1980-1981 expenditures in higher education will reach $43.5 billion in 1970-1971 dollars (National Center for Educational Statistics, 1973, pp. 99-101).

Higher education has social importance not only because it consumes a large amount of resources but also because it benefits society as a whole as well as individuals who are fortunate enough to receive instruction in colleges and universities. What social benefits are currently produced in our colleges and universities? First, institutions of higher education are responsible for the creation of new knowledge through their research activities. They also help to develop the capacity of individuals to create new knowledge, even if these individuals choose to carry on their research outside a university setting. Persons who engage in research do not claim for themselves the full value of the knowledge they create, for new knowledge increases the welfare of all individuals in a society.

Second, higher education helps maintain social continuity. While many people have found much to criticize in our government and in our society generally, especially in recent years, few people favor ripping the existing social fabric asunder. There is a negative association between years of schooling and antisocial behavior, although many other factors complicate this relationship. For example, according to the report of the Senate Select Committee on Equal Educational Opportunity, "The costs to the nation of crime that is related to inadequate education appears to be about $3 billion *a year* and rising" (U.S. Congress, 1972). (This estimate is based on a study made for the committee by Levin, 1972.) Furthermore, "evidence is accumulating that the educational attainment of the mother is among the most important determinants of a child's future academic and economic success. The education of women enhances the educability of the next generation and . . . [increases] the efficiency of the family as an institution which helps to maintain the continuity of the social order" (Nerlove, 1972, S194-S195).

Third, society benefits from the "ranking" or "sorting" function of higher education: matching students' interests and aptitudes to their careers. In formal education, primary schools are responsible for guiding and nurturing talent. The process of matching individual talents to careers, however, is not completed even by the end of secondary school. College admissions procedures, counseling services, the wide variety of undergraduate courses, and graduate and professional school admissions procedures all have a part to play in the sorting process. This process has both costs and benefits. The costs are heavy when matching is biased against students of low socioeconomic status or of minority race, but we all benefit when poets, doctors, mathematicians, and environmental scientists are, by aptitude and training, well skilled to work in these particular fields.

One would expect individuals to benefit from the sorting function through increases in their income. But they also benefit from the fact that educational institutions have no interest in keeping test results secret. If employers were engaged in testing and sorting activities, many of them would probably want to keep the results secret in order to hold competitive advantage in salary negotiations with talented new employees and to reduce the effectiveness of rival attempts to bid away their best workers.

Fourth, higher education helps broaden the market for books, music, other works of art, and a variety of forms of human communication (Weisbrod, 1964, p. 33). This wide market, in turn, offers economies of scale in the production of books, in the performance of symphonies, operas, and popular music, and in the provision of virtually all types of communication. Lower prices resulting from economies of scale allow people of widely differing income levels to participate in the intellectual activities that appeal to them.

Fifth and last, turning back to the question of economic productivity, we recognize that even when persons are able to seize the full monetary value of any added productivity they have acquired through higher education, they may still generate economic benefits that spill over to other workers, if not to citizens in general. This is likely to happen whenever the productivity of one employee depends on the productivity of others. Given the realities of industrialization, this interdependence of worker productivity occurs quite frequently (Cohn, 1972, pp. 128-129).

The financing of activities that produce social benefits is grounded in compulsory levies because it is impossible to exclude a noncontributor from the benefits intended for all society. It would be unthinkable, for example, to finance national defense through voluntary contributions because the amount of protection a person received would not be measurably affected by the size of the person's contribution. Therefore, no one would voluntarily make any contribution. Precisely the same argument applies to medical research and the training of medical researchers, activities conducted largely by universities. However, people willingly vote for taxation to finance social benefits because the benefits are valuable and because each person knows that others are required to pay their fair share of the costs.

Public subsidies may be justified however not only on the basis of social benefits as conventionally defined, but on the basis of fairness or equity. The concept of fairness has been commented on by Rawls (1971, p. 250), who observes, "The force of justice as fairness would appear to arise from two things: the requirement that *all inequalities be justified to the least advantaged,* and the priority of liberty" (italics added).

Different justifications for public support direct subsidies toward different recipients, institutions and students alike. For example, the social-benefit justification for subsidy is consistent with the distribution of educational grants to students according to their ability; those who have strong academic talents and who are willing to work hard are more likely to produce the sorts of social benefits we have discussed than are students with little talent and energy. A related line of argument would direct institutional subsidies toward major universities because major universities attract a disproportionate share of highly talented and well motivated students.

The fairness criterion, however, might demand equal subsidies per student—or per college-age person. It could be argued that the measurement of social benefits is not sufficiently precise, either theoretically or empirically, to warrant unequal treatment. The preferred policy even might be to subsidize students in inverse measure to their academic abilities. At the same time, nonstudents might be given cash payments equal to student subsidies, which they could use as they wished instead of investing in their own training. "One should recognize that the poorest among us, and the one most deserving of help from his fellowmen, is the one whom nature forgot to endow with brains—and that the way to make it up to him is not to exclude him from school and tax him to pay part of the cost of educating his intellectually well-endowed and no-longer-poor peer group . . . , but to give him money in lieu of the brains he lacks" (Johnson, 1972, p. S289).

Alternatively, it may be desired to distribute educational resources to reduce the range of incomes in our society or to break the relationship between the income and education levels of parents and the education of children. Children from wealthy and well-educated families take disproportionate advantage of educational opportunities (Anderson, Bowman, and Tinto, 1972, pp. 272-274). Furthermore, evidence shows that the pattern of public subsidies of higher education actually distributes income from poor to middle class (Hansen and Weisbrod, 1969).

Educational grants to improve the distribution of income would direct public subsidies toward children from poor families. Such grants would effect a redistribution of present resources by placing the tax burden primarily on middle- and upper-income families, while recipients of the funds would be primarily poor families. The grants would be intended as well to produce a new distribution of lifetime earnings favoring children from poor families. Education is an especially effective tool in such redistribution compared with other forms of public subsidy, for it cannot easily be lost or taken away. It is peculiarly a lifetime asset. (Education alone, however, may not be of much help in the short run in improving the job and income prospects of the ghetto poor. Deliberate action to open up new job markets in central city areas may be necessary as well—Harrison, 1972, pp. 796-811.) Considerations of equity, therefore, lead us to prefer progressive rather than regressive policies both for taxation to support higher education and for making opportunities for higher education fully available to poor youth.

In general, social benefits are distributed broadly through

the society and cannot be claimed exclusively by any one individual, not even that individual most closely associated with
their production. Hence, they are external to private production
and use and are frequently referred to as *externalities* of higher
education. Of course, not all yields of higher education are
external to the student who attends a college or university. For
example, the number of years of higher education a person
completes is positively associated with his or her earned income.
And as the average number of school and college years completed by each new entrant to the labor force rises, national
product rises also, all other things being equal. This gain is not
ordinarily viewed as a social benefit. But education does much
more than increase the productive capacity of individuals. It
enhances the capacity of the individual to understand society
and participate in all kinds of cultural activities. Thus, for the
individual, education offers two benefits—it enhances his or her
capacity as a "consumer" to participate in avocational interests,
and it increases his or her capacity as a "producer" to function
in the labor force.

Economists have had little success in measuring the value
to an individual of the consumption, or life-enhancing, aspect of
education. But economists can assess the contribution of education to the development of an individual's work skills by relating earnings to the amount and type of education a person has
received. On the average, medical doctors earn more money
than people who conclude their formal education at the baccau-
laureate level. The extra, or differential, earned income of
physicians can thus be attributed to the extra amount of education they have received. The phrase *on the average,* is important, for some doctors earn more than others, and to some
extent differences in earnings among doctors may be related to
personal characteristics, not to an extra amount or better quality of education received. It is the broadly measured difference
in income over education categories that enters into economists'
calculations.

Because income is received over a considerable period,
comparing the earnings of different groups of people becomes
complicated. Two individuals with the same amount and type

of education may earn their peak incomes at quite different points in their life cycles. Consider two graduates of a liberal arts college. One, a successful football player, is likely to have peak income around age thirty, while the other, an insurance agent, may reach peak income in his middle to late fifties. Economists would say that even if the total lifetime earnings of these two people are equal in absolute dollar amounts, the football player, nevertheless, has a higher lifetime income because money earns money. To compare income among groups of individuals, the economist computes the present discounted value of their incomes and obtains a single-valued estimate of their worth by dividing the actual or expected earnings in each future year by a standard interest rate raised to the power of years as calculated from the year of initial earnings. Clearly, as the year in which the income is to be received is farther distant and the standard interest rate is higher, the present discounted value of that income is lowered.

We have suggested that there are good and sufficient reasons to be concerned about efficiency in higher education. The chapters that follow discuss criteria for judging various aspects of efficiency in our colleges and universities. Economic efficiency is judged by the degree to which institutions of higher education employ their considerable resources to provide us with services we highly value. Technological efficiency is attained as maximum yield toward objectives is drawn from any given amount of expenditure, which is to say, simply, that wastefulness in instruction and research is thoroughly avoided. Fiscal efficiency is a matter of maximizing private contributions for the support of higher education relative to compulsory levies. Social efficiency is based on maximizing educational opportunities so that talent and interest, rather than parental or personal income, determine access. We examine in the chapters that follow the various means by which economic, financial, technical, and social efficiency can be enhanced.

Berkeley, California　　　　　　　　Charles S. Benson
February 1974　　　　　　　　　　Harold L. Hodgkinson

Contents

Implementing the Learning Society

NEW STRATEGIES FOR FINANCING SOCIAL OBJECTIVES

1

Creating High-Level Manpower

Economic efficiency is the fitting of the character and quantity of products or outputs to demand. In broadest terms, it determines whether people are getting what they want from an economic activity. In private markets, competition is expected to hold entrepreneurs to reasonable standards of economic efficiency. In order to make profits, firms must respond to household tastes and turn out salable products.

In the public sector, it is not always easy to judge what people want or accurately describe the products of complex public institutions such as state universities. Most colleges and universities have characteristics of both competitive businesses and public institutions. They try to make their programs of study appeal to both the vocational and nonvocational interests of students and to offer satisfactory living conditions; otherwise they will not attract the caliber of students they want. Because students in higher education are not bound by district lines to attend an institution in their immediate geographic area, this pressure toward economic efficiency affects public institutions as well as private. Colleges and universities also try to prepare their graduates for their chosen lines of work or for graduate or professional study as completely as rival institutions. If the quality of output slips at any institution, talented persons will no longer apply for admission and a cycle of deterioration may set in.

1

In most institutions, however, faculty hold much decision-making power, which they exercise without any serious
assessment of consumer tastes. To this extent, institutions stand
apart from competitive forces. For example, faculty in an institution may decide on rates of expansion for graduate and professional programs without taking into account the need of the
economy for graduates from particular programs. Program em-
phases—whether, for example, the department of city and regional planning should emphasize physical design or environment problems—may be set simply according to the academic
interests of staff members. Likewise, decisions on the future
directions of basic research are frequently made by senior faculty without outside counsel. Actions of funding agencies—the
federal government, state governments, foundations, large business firms (in contracting for research), or private donors—influence what faculty and students do, but it is risky to assert that
the pressures they apply reveal a national or regional consensus
on what outputs are desired of higher education or that such a
consensus even exists.

Introduction

What should the size and scope of student enrollment in
higher education be? The range of opinion on this question is
still wide. Fritz Machlup (1971, p. 6) holds an elitist view:
"Higher education is too high for the average intelligence, much
too high for the average interest, and vastly too high for the
average patience and perseverance of the people, here or anywhere. Attempts to expose from 30 to 50 percent of the people
to higher education are completely useless." Plainly, Machlup
would ration places in higher education on the basis of intellectual aptitudes and interests, which is not the same as rationing
them on the basis of family background. In the last class to be
selected for Princeton before the outbreak of World War II, the
class of 1943, approximately 450 persons, or about 80 perent
of the class, were graduates of preparatory schools. Such
schools are expensive, exclusive, and supposedly dedicated to
the intellectual life, but upon graduation the class offered the
following: favorite novel, *Gone With the Wind*; favorite poem,
"If," by Kipling; favorite play, *Man Who Came to Dinner* (*King*

Lear was second choice). In the postwar years, Princeton has become larger, more democratic, and coeducational; it has also become vastly more intellectual.

At the other extreme, both New York City and the State of California offer high school graduates open admissions to colleges and universities within their systems and charge minimum fees (the City University of New York charges no tuition fees to fulltime matriculated students who are residents of New York City; California charges no tuition fees in its junior colleges, which generally offer only lower division programs). According to CUNY (1972), "free public schools have come to be an accepted fact, viewed as essential to economic growth and stability, representing the best road for the escape from poverty for millions of Americans through generations of our history. . . . Just as the demands of our economy required high school training a generation ago, today college education has become a basic requirement for meaningful employment in hundreds of occupations." Although it has been argued that this is an artificial requirement for many occupations, under such an expansionist view, the size of enrollment in higher education would depend solely on the desires of college-age youth to attend— neither fees nor rigorous entrance requirements would stand in their way. This is called the social demand approach.

Between the elitist and the expansionist views stands the possibility of relying on the market to determine the size of higher education enrollments more specifically than simply declaring, as CUNY does, that times have changed and many occupations now require college degrees. In 1935, Walsh suggested that college enrollments expand up to the point where differential income associated with postsecondary education, at present discounted value, was equal to the cost of acquiring that education, counting the student's foregone income as an element of cost. In his empirical studies Walsh found that the private or individual returns of education exceeded private costs. Arguing that one man's income is another man's expense, Walsh saw the highly educated enjoying a monopoly profit; they could sell their services for value in excess of the cost of producing additional educated persons. Because of the law of diminishing marginal returns, the expansion of higher education, by producing more graduates, would drive down the prices paid for the services of college-trained persons. Expansion might also raise the cost per student of higher education, but eventually there would be an equilibrium point at which the private returns from college and university studies would equal private costs.

Danière (1964, 24-25) has indicated that equilibrium may be reached at a point where the discounted value of returns is less than costs, because education offers consumption benefits as well as vocational benefits. "As enrollment expands," he writes, "the differential income to be expected from education will fall. Even after it has dropped to equality with cost, new purchasers will appear since the sum of all benefits (income plus direct consumption) is still worth more than cost. So the market expands further, income expectations will sink below cost, the difference between cost and income representing a positive (and increasing) 'net price' of direct consumption benefits. The market will stabilize at the point where further purchases would drive the net price of these benefits beyond anyone's evaluation of their worth." This argument assumes that production and consumption aspects of education cannot be separately produced—or that institutions would be unwilling to sell them separately even if it were possible.

In a strict and rigorous interpretation, regulation of the size of higher education enrollment by allowing an equilibrium to be established between private returns and costs ignores the social benefits of education. Depending on whether plans for deferred financing are made available and how they are constructed, full-cost pricing, as this approach is called, may or may not be consistent with the criteria of fairness and income redistribution. Strict full-cost pricing would also raise barriers to the education of women as long as they carry disproportionately heavy responsibility for the care of their household and children, or until they are paid for it according to the level of their education.

How should enrollments in different departments, specialties, and professional schools be determined? Enrollments in higher education are widely distributed among different departments and programs. Under the criterion of economic efficiency, this distribution must reflect accurately the demands of the consumers of higher education. But who are these consumers? Considering that the function of higher education is to create trained manpower, consumers are the members of every household in the nation. Thus institutions should ensure that educational resources are distributed among departments, programs, and so on, to achieve a balance between the demand for and the supply of different types of manpower (Organization for Economic Cooperation and Development, 1970). Colleges and universities should help overcome bottlenecks in the demand for persons with different occupational skills and professional specialties and at the same time avoid turning out persons who cannot find employment in the work they have been trained for. Later, we will explore some of the difficulties of estimating future demands for various types of manpower. However, work affords satisfactions beyond income, and the worker has the right to choose his trade. Hence, it might be said that students should be able to crowd up in certain occupations and accept the resulting declining wage levels if they wish.

But individual students are also interested in education as a form of consumption, for they attend colleges and universities not simply to acquire work skills but to achieve greater understanding of the arts, the intellect, and culture. For the most part, however, beyond the most basic levels of instruction, such benefits of consumption are by-products of vocational interests. For example, a math major may take a course in the painting of the High Renaissance to satisfy his demand for education as consumption, even though the course is presumably offered to prepare people to be art historians.

A related question is whether a proper range of courses to satisfy the consumption demand for education is available for people at the age, time, or place it is convenient for them. Although university extension services seek to meet this demand, it is not at all clear whether institutions devote enough resources to such activities.

How should budgetary resources be distributed between instruction and research? The two main functions of higher education are instruction and research. To a degree the two functions are complementary; certain instruction requires a research program and certain research naturally results in instruction (Nerlove, 1972, pp. S199-S201). We will return to this point in Chapter Two.

Institutions maintain wide discretion for the proper allocation of resources between research and instruction. The criterion of economic efficiency demands that these choices reflect the desires of consumers, the members of the households of the nation. However, research scientists will maintain that the general public is ill-equipped to evaluate the potential yield and significance of research, especially basic research. Moreover, the incentive structure for faculty appointments and promotions tends to favor research, though incentives are likely to change as faculties become unionized. A questioning public mood about the yield and cost-effectiveness of research might cause faculty and their scientist colleagues in government to lose the power of determining the size of research programs (Walsh, 1971, pp. 459-463).

How should resources be distributed *among different subjects of research*? The public probably has less to say about the allocation of university research budgets than about any other question under the topic of economic efficiency. Since the total university research budget is the sum of the amounts spent in different departments and programs, this and the previous question cannot easily be separated.

Initiative about the funding of research activities may rest with bodies that supply the money—government, the foundations, or large corporations—when the university, on behalf of a department or institute, contracts to supply research services. Initiative may also come from faculty members who make research proposals to sponsoring bodies, including the university administration itself. In some cases, the cost of research, taking into account available library facilities, may not exceed the value of the faculty member's own time; since the faculty member often controls the use of his time over and beyond that which he spends in teaching, he has the power in such a case individually to decide upon his research priorities.

It is important to note that the public is seldom consulted about research priorities. Where no outside funding is involved and a project is under the control of a single faculty member, he is likely to claim the privilege of academic freedom and pursue his studies as he sees fit. When major funding is required, research scientists claim authority to decide which projects are pushed forward and which are turned aside. For example, when the federal government is dividing up its research budget in any field, it invites scientists from the field to advise it on spending strategies and specific projects. Scientists can claim that only they—certainly not the public—can estimate the success or significance of particular methods of research and the competence of their colleagues.

Success in research, especially if it is newsworthy, stimulates the flow of research funds. If success is achieved by an American, hope for additional breakthroughs is raised. If success is achieved by a foreign rival, envy and national pride release a flow of money. Aside from recognizing these demonstration effects, it is difficult for the ordinary citizen to predict the scale, direction, or effects on his own life of future research activities. This is unfortunate but probably inevitable. Yet as political processes become more effective in defining national objectives, university research will be more likely to meet those objectives in an economically efficient manner. In its dealings with universities, the federal government, the major source of research funds in the United States, is now shifting its attention away from medical research and toward environmental problems. Presumably, this change is based on a redefinition of national priorities. On the basis of the public's right to know, scientists should make more effort to inform the public of the problems and difficulties they face and the progress of research in different areas.

The system of higher education in the United States operates in the virtual absence of a national education policy. Without such a policy, how can we then obtain a proper balance between the demand for and the supply of specific types of highly educated persons? The traditional answer to this question is that the market for human services functions so that persons are allowed to make the "right choices" in selecting their programs of study, and that institutions respond quickly to these market-generated shifts in student demand for different instructional programs. For example, if there were a shortage of architects at the same time there were an oversupply of civil engineers, then the salaries offered to newly trained architects would rise, while the beginning pay of civil engineers would fall. Moreover, young architects would gain rapid promotion for satisfactory work, but newly trained civil engineers would find themselves consigned to tasks that formerly had been performed by technicians. News of these conditions in the labor market would spread to undergraduates, so economic theory has it, shaping their occupational plans. They would eagerly seek places in architectural programs at colleges and universities, and the average caliber of applicants would rise. (However, some evidence indicates that students do not necessarily respond to changes in the present value of lifetime earnings for graduates from particular departments by enrolling in those departments. See Klinov-Malul, 1971.) Just the opposite would happen in civil engineering programs. Faculties in architecture would use the evidence of demand for their programs to plead for expansion; civil engineering faculties would find themselves in a poor bargaining position for intrauniversity allocations of resources. The final outcome of the process would be that the supply of newly trained architects would increase while that of civil engineers would fall. The process would continue until equilibrium in the labor market was restored.

Equilibrium of prices of different types of labor, defined as a wage rate established by the intersection of demand and supply schedules for specific sorts of employees, is subject to a variety of economic forces. On the supply side, the schedule (which relates numbers of qualified persons who offer their services to changes in wage levels) depends on the relative degree of scarcity of inherent skills, on the length, cost, and rigor of required training, on the general views of the relative attractiveness of the given line of work (determined in part by location, hours, pace, noise, and so forth, and in part by traditional views of its status), on the prospects for stability of tenure on the one hand and advancement on the other, and on individual autonomy in determining one's conditions of work. Demand reflects consumers' preferences for goods and services of the given industry, physical capital per worker, rate of technological advance, and so on. Both demand and supply are influenced in the real world by monopolistic powers.

Planning

The rationale for relying upon the market to direct and control the creation of high-level manpower is based on the assumption that household preferences for different kinds of goods and services and student preferences for different kinds of careers can and should regulate the production of our most economically significant resource, labor in all its forms. We have an extremely decentralized arrangement to determine the salable products of higher education.

Not all countries proceed in the same way. An example of a different approach is found in the Soviet Union, where education planning and manpower planning are two aspects of a unified process (De Witt, 1967, pp. 220, 226).

> Since 1928 the guiding policy in allocating scarce resources to education has been the recognition by the Soviet government of what are commonly called "bottleneck problems" of cadres of qualified manpower whose training required "some time" (from a few months to many years)—the shortfall of which impeded specific development projects. . . . [The planning of human resource allocation begins with the computation of "labor balances," a] chessboard method of ascertaining for each sector, industry, and occupation where people are presently employed and where additions to the current stocks should be obtained. In short, a "labor balance" is simply the physical allocation of manpower resources by sectors, industries, occupations, types of education, and regional units. It is only after the physical allocation has been made—how many youths are needed to enter gainful employment and how many will be allowed to continue a given type of education—that the educational au-

thorities enter the scene and begin "planning" for
the required number of admissions for study by
specialty and type of training.

Labor balances are developed for long-range plans extending ten
to twenty years into the future, for middle-range plans of five
to seven years, and for annual plans. Data obtained in the com-
putation of annual plans are used to make necessary revisions in
the middle- and long-range forecasts. There is, therefore, a con-
tinuous process of revision in forecasting labor requirements
and recognizing private household demand for the quantity and
type of education. Ultimately, the set of labor balances is "used
in planning the size of enrollment of students in higher and
secondary specialized educational establishments, in vocational-
technical colleges and secondary schools of general education,
and also in fixing the amount of labor to be recruited and of
population to be resettled" (Nozhko and others, 1968, p. 91).
    Most Americans would prefer that choices of education,
training, occupation, and region of residence not be subject to
such close control by central authorities. This is not to say that
our present laissez-faire approach to economic efficiency in
higher education works faultlessly or that increased use of manpower forecasting techniques, and related techniques of estimating the economic values of alternative types of higher education, is inappropriate in our own country.
    One difficulty in relying heavily on market mechanisms
to control the flow of graduates is that of time lags. Returning
to our example of a shortage of architects and a surplus of civil
engineers, it would almost certainly take a while for businesses
to recognize the existence of such a shortage or surplus. An
architectural firm in a busy time would sign new contracts and
plan to expand its staff in order to meet them. The firm would
explore the market for architects through, say, the conventional
channels of university recruitment and advertising. It might
then explore the possibility of raiding the staffs of rival firms
and of upgrading junior or nonprofessional staff in its own
ranks. When executives in a number of firms in a certain geographic area concluded that they were unable to find staff to

meet their contracts, starting salaries for new architects would be likely to rise. (For an overall discussion of the problem of time lag in the adjustment of wages, see Arrow and Capron, 1959, pp. 292-308.)

It would require additional time for the word about salaries and job openings to get to college placement offices and undergraduates. And then the process of training itself would consume time—perhaps two to four years. The expansion of training programs might require new facilities and new faculty. In the meantime, employer firms might realize that the shortage was more serious and persistent than they first thought and might raise starting salaries a second or third time. These signals from the market would induce yet another round of training expansion.

At some point, a stream of additional newly trained architects would enter the market—to find, perhaps, that job openings had dried up. In the four to ten years since the shortage was first recognized, the demand for new housing may have slumped—and with it the demand for new architects. Alternatively, the fact that employers failed to realize that the production of new staff required time and therefore gave repeated, duplicate signals of shortage to colleges and universities may have led institutions to expand architectural programs more than the original situation called for. Finally, once colleges and universities geared up to meet the new demand for highly trained persons, it would be difficult to reduce the size of the affected programs until evidence accumulated from the market that a surplus, rather than a shortage, existed. Because it takes time for evidence of a surplus to present itself, it would be almost certain that a high outflow of graduates would continue beyond the point of peak demand. This time-lag phenomenon explains, in part, the excess of space scientists and engineers in the early 1970s.

Employment in public and quasi-public activities (including colleges and universities) is unlikely to generate accurate signals with regard to current manpower requirements. In most countries, governments are the largest single employers of educated manpower, yet they ordinarily pay their employees on the basis of paper qualifications and seniority, not productivity. For example, the rates of pay of school teachers continues to advance in the United States even though we have an unparalleled oversupply of qualified applicants. As Blaug (1972, p. 61) says, "If the private sector sets the rate of pay for the public sector, the fact that the marginal product of labor is difficult to define in the public sector will reflect the marginal revenue product of labor in the economy. But the public sector may decide to pay more than the marginal revenue product of labor to ease its recruitment problems . . . or to pay less to create employment opportunities. Our only test of 'more or less' is the marginal product of labor in the private sectors. The concept of marginal productivity has no meaning in the public sector, not so much because the government does not sell its output . . . but because governments are not profit maximizers."

Signals from the public sector to students and society about requirements for trained manpower in the public sector are also made difficult to interpret because training for public employment is often subsidized to a greater degree than is training in general. Yet the government is in a better position than private employers to estimate its future needs (Layard, 1972). In short, there is a strong case for serious governmental efforts to forecast the requirements of the public sector and to make use of such estimates to inform students, institutions, and the public.

Let us consider in detail manpower production for the largest consumer of skills within the public sector, the education enterprise, dealing first with elementary and secondary schoolteachers. In 1972, the New York State Commission on the Quality, Cost, and Financing of Elementary and Secondary Education (the Fleischmann Commission) drew attention to the fact that in 1970 the state issued provisional certificates (that is, certificates granted to newly trained prospective teachers) to over twice as many persons as could be employed in its public and private schools—34,000 certificates compared with an upper estimate of 15,700 available jobs. The commission noted that if past trends in teacher preparation were maintained, there would be an excess of more than 185,000 teachers between

1971 and 1984. New York is a progressive state in education policy, but the teacher surplus seems to have caught it by surprise. In the City University of New York, the ratio of teacher-education graduates who had obtained teaching jobs by October 1 of their graduation year fell from 75.2 percent in 1970 to 50.1 percent in 1971 (New York State Commission on the Quality, Cost, and Financing of Elementary and Secondary Education, 1972). Upstate institutions responded to the situation by halting the training of elementary schoolteachers altogether—possibly an extreme reaction although no growth in elementary school enrollment, the primary determinant of demand, was expected during the 1970s.

Projections of requirements for schoolteachers are relatively easy to make. Demand may conveniently be separated into that created by new openings and that created by replacement needs. The number of openings is a function of enrollment and class size. Since elementary and most of secondary education is compulsory, enrollment is then determined by the size of the school-age population. The number of school-age children is almost automatically predictable over ten-year periods because the class to enter school five years hence has already been born and because birth rates change only gradually. Class size likewise changes only gradually. If major alterations in class size are intended, however, these can be built into the forecasting model. Teacher replacement demand is somewhat more difficult to estimate. Data are required on age distributions of teachers, their sex, recent turnover patterns according to age and sex, and the propensity of former teachers to return to service after a period at home or in another line of work (New York State Commission on the Quality, Cost, and Financing of Elementary and Secondary Education, 1972).

The failure of institutions to anticipate changes in requirements for a major occupational group such as schoolteachers can have unfortunate consequences. Young people who have completed their training and cannot find work as teachers naturally are disappointed. The taxpayer may feel that the state has been wasteful in training persons for nonexistent jobs. The severe cutbacks that are likely to follow from unanticipated surpluses fall heavily on members of minority groups, for these groups are just now gaining a foothold in many professions, including teaching.

Proper forecasting of manpower requirements can bring to light desirable policy options. In times of surplus, teacher training institutions can be encouraged to make their training intensive by requiring additional years of study; they can also be encouraged to shift temporarily from training new teachers to continuing the education of older teachers.

The failure of the market to adjust supply to demand is apparent not just with respect to total numbers of teachers but also with respect to their specialties. For twenty years the National Education Association (1972) has noted a surplus of teachers certified in the social sciences and a shortage in mathematics, yet the situation continues. In this instance, any correction by market forces is bound to be slight since teachers generally are unwilling to accept the notion that persons who work in undersupplied fields should receive higher pay, and school districts are willing to convert social science teachers into mathematics teachers simply by administrative fiat.

In the case of college faculty, a similar surplus has developed. Early warning of this surplus was given by Cartter (1965), whose findings showed that the seller's market in higher education was likely to disappear within a decade.

The size of the college-age population in the United States will almost certainly decline absolutely in the decade of the 1980s; the rate of increase is already declining. According to the acceleration principle, demand for faculty is sensitive to changes in the rate of expansion or contraction of student enrollments, and student enrollments are based on changes in the size of college-age population. The present surplus is a result of past high rates of expansion in Ph.D. production and a slackening in the rate of growth of student enrollments.

Absolute decreases in numbers of college-age youth during the 1980s will affect college enrollments, though whether enrollments themselves will decline absolutely or simply level out is a matter of dispute (Balderston and Radner, 1971). During the coming decade, academic demand for new Ph.D.s will depend largely on efforts made to improve the caliber of teaching staff in four-year undergraduate programs. How intensive an effort will be made will be determined by the adequacy of financing, and as yet we have no way to estimate long-term financial commitments to higher education.

In any case, changes in wage rates will not be effective in clearing the market for Ph.D.s in the years ahead. Wage rates would be effective if a projected drop in earnings led prospective Ph.D.s to seek other training or if the lower salaries being offered to Ph.D.s led employers to hire more of them; but these kinds of responses would probably not be substantial except in the unlikely event of a large drop in salaries. Persons who enter graduate schools are attracted to a field of study and to a particular life style. Salary is only a part of the work bargain they hope to make and, in many cases, not an important part. Colleges and universities, moreover, are not inclined to force new faculty to accept conditions of penury even when there is a surplus of candidates, for to do so would distract new faculty from doing their work properly and thus represent a false economy. At worst, then, the lucky few who found employment in universities and colleges would face only a modest relative decline in living standard compared with that which they would enjoy if the market for academic talent were tight.

Does unemployment among Ph.D.s discourage persons from seeking enrollment in graduate schools? No doubt it discourages some, but plainly not enough to bring the supply of graduates into line with demand. Given the chance to study the subjects which interest them, quite possibly with subsidized fees, and given even a small chance of obtaining a faculty post, many young people choose to spend several years as graduate students as long as openings are available in university programs.

Market adjustments to a surplus in Ph.D. supply are imperfect, not only because salaries are administered, but also because this stickiness of salaries (and the failure of salary changes to curb enrollment) is combined with a time-lag problem. Balderston and Radner (1971, pp. 50-51) set up a hypothetical situation to describe the problem. They imagine that an institution of higher education wishes to begin a set of new doctoral programs as soon as it can. In the early 1970s it took action to appoint committees of key faculty to design new curricula. A year or two later a new program could begin to enroll students.

> Meanwhile, efforts would be made to lure a few "star" faculty to attract other more junior faculty and to serve also as a basis for attracting research funds from extramural sources. Along the way, perhaps at the time the new program is announced, the plans would be firm enough to show that a new building was needed for the program and to commence the planning and the effort to acquire funding for it. Five years after this decision, a new building would actually be on-stream and operating, so that a definite expansion of the doctoral program's enrollment could not occur. But it is now *1978*. An enlarged class of new graduate students, entering in that year, would come on the market in 1984, a year of absolutely negative academic demand for new Ph.D.'s—and, they would all have to wait until 1988 to have a prayer of a chance of an academic position. . . . Clearly, if this is a trustworthy picture of the future, it would be very unwise for the institution to start, in 1971, with the sequence of efforts and decisions which would produce such a catastrophe for it and its students in the mid-1980s.

Yet competitive pressure toward institution-building is leading middle-level universities to expand their doctoral programs even today.

The implications of these actions are clear. In the absence of centralized directives on manpower requirements from the federal government, a decentralized system of higher education is likely to produce periodic surpluses of highly trained manpower—holders of Ph.D.s and other advanced degrees. More than merely providing information about occupational trends, centralized directives would reinforce such information with effective incentives for institutions, students, or both. But several unfortunate consequences might follow. First, graduates might feel frustrated and take obstructionist actions through

political channels. Second, those who provided support to higher education, either through paying taxes or making gifts, might
come to feel that their money was being wasted and seek to cut
off the flow. Third, worthwhile new programs might be fore-
stalled or aborted because of the difficulties of placing graduates when supply was expanding too rapidly. Fourth, postgradu-
ate programs might shift too completely into the hands of sec-
ond- and third-rate institutions as first-rate ones cut back enrollments to maintain placement standards. Fifth, eventual over-
reaction to the surplus might lead to severe cutbacks in almost
all institutions, with the result that after a period of time severe
shortages of highly trained manpower would show up again;
that is, a stop-and-go process of dealing with graduate and professional enrollments would develop, seriously out of phase
with the changes in the need for trained persons.

The arguments in this chapter suggest that the economic
efficiency of colleges and universities might be enhanced if the
sizes of programs were related through positive action to requirements for different types of graduates. This argument assumes that techniques exist to determine our future requirements. We stress the word *future* because instruction takes
years, and occupational skills, once acquired, are supposed to
last a person throughout his working life. In the next section we
consider possible techniques for estimating these manpower requirements.

Estimating Needs

Two techniques are currently used to estimate manpower
needs: projections of manpower requirements and cost-benefit
analysis. For projecting manpower requirements there are two
subtechniques: drawing projections from existing manpower
utilization within a given country and making international
comparisons.

As developed by Parnes (1962), there are several steps in
the first process. First, it is necessary to prepare a manpower
inventory, showing labor force participation by age and sex,
rates of unemployment, and the occupational distribution of

workers by industry, age and sex, and educational level. Where possible, changes over time are shown.

Next, a forecast of the future size of the labor force is prepared. This work begins with making simple population forecasts by age and sex and then uses data from the manpower inventory to compute labor force participation rates by age and sex and apply them to the population projections.

Then a projection of GNP is made. Estimates of the future size of GNP (ordinarily five, ten, and twenty years ahead) should be consistent with projections of the size of the labor force, unemployment rates, the length of the work week and work year, and output per worker (labor productivity).

These GNP projections are divided into the real money value of output in each industrial sector, such as agriculture, mining, manufacturing, and trade, and these values, together with interindustry estimates of output per worker, are translated into estimates of gross employment in different industries. Data from the manpower inventory are used to assign the gross estimates of labor in the different industries to occupational categories (scientist, draftsman, salesman, skilled machinist, operator).

Educational qualifications for the different occupational categories are established, based mainly on the existing practices as revealed in the manpower inventory. Needs for newly trained persons at different levels and with different educational qualifications are estimated from this data, together with estimates of qualified persons now in the labor force adjusted to reflect projected retirements, withdrawals, deaths, and so on. Thus the net requirements for newly trained persons are computed by taking into account new places plus replacement demand for persons who will leave the labor force. Obviously, the data from the manpower inventory are helpful in estimating replacement demand.

Few countries have enough detailed, accurate data to carry out this manpower forecasting exercise properly, but the basic scheme has been used in most Mediterranean countries and in less developed regions. Though the procedures are straightforward, they have come under serious attack.

First, there is as yet no reasonable way to estimate future changes in productivity, making the process of forecasting future occupational structure difficult.

Second, there is little hard knowledge about the amount and type of education required to carry out a particular occupational assignment. Thus, single estimates of future needs for persons with a given type of schooling are subject to extreme error. Consider a country that on grounds of meeting great social demand for education and increasing opportunities for minorities opens wide the doors to community colleges. Community college graduates eventually would find jobs, though possibly at lower rates of pay than they had expected. They probably would displace high school graduates in the job market, even though their additional two years of education might not enhance the effective level of applied skills in the industry. An employer might prefer to hire community college graduates instead of high school graduates because they were simply available, because they did not cost much more than high school graduates, or because they increased the prestige of the firm. If this change occurred, the manpower planner would begin to make his projections as if community college education were required for work formerly done by less educated persons. Thus, once the training-occupation nexus became disordered, the manpower analyst would project that disorder into the future and seek to perpetuate it.

Third, manpower analysts give little if any attention to the substitution of one type of labor or professional skill for another or to substitutions between different types of physical capital and labor. In the real world, one would expect changes in relative supplies of different types of labor to influence wage and salary levels, and—taking into account the costs in both money and effort of acquiring different skills—changes in wage and salary levels should influence the willingness of people to enter different kinds of training programs. By and large, manpower forecasting does not take into account these shifts made in response to changes in so-called opportunity costs, but they are central to economic thinking (Hollister, 1967).

The second method of projecting manpower requirements, making international comparisons, can be dealt with briefly. The analyst accumulates data on the educational levels of workers in a set of countries. He or she then relates for each country the reliance on educated persons to such variables as total population, GNP, GNP per capita, and the rates of change in such variables. Multiple regression analysis, a statistical technique used to show the average effects of one set of variables on another set, as well as to reveal the closeness or precision of the relationship, is used to establish the relationship between educational requirements and various national characteristics.

Using such procedures, Rado and Jolly (1968, pp. 76-97) suggest that the demand for college and university graduates in any country may be estimated by the formula $r_G = 1.038 \times r_I + 0.164 \times r_P$, where r is rate of change, G is demand for graduates, I is national income, and P is population. Rado and Jolly recognize, however, that "manpower planning, as it is practiced today, is a bastard child of economics. It counts men against output rather than benefits against costs; it implicitly assumes that the production function, from which the demand for graduates is derived, permits no substitution of one factor for another when relative factor prices change, hence the demand for graduates is not a function of their price" (p. 76).

The international comparisons approach is subject to the same general criticisms as are projections derived from the existing pattern of utilization of labor skills of one country, and it has one other: Because there is no discernible pattern of utilization of education and skills among nations, conclusions drawn from assumed relationships between levels of development of countries and their need for educated persons are subject to extremely large statistical errors (Weathersby, 1972).

The cost-benefit method of educational planning assumes a high degree of substitution of labor. Accordingly, the policy recommendations that flow from cost-benefit analysis are aimed at increasing the supply of any form of skilled manpower for which lifetime earnings appear to be high compared with the educational costs of creating the skills. An increase in the relative supply of unusually scarce skills will bring down wages and salaries earned by persons who have those skills; correspondingly, any diversion of students into undermanned fields means a reduction of surplus skills, so that earnings in fields which formerly had labor surpluses should rise. Equilibrium will be approached when the differences in lifetime earnings for different occupations precisely reflect the differences in costs of acquiring the necessary skills to enter these fields.

Recent evidence indicates that salaries and wages respond highly to changes in the relative supply of different skills. From such evidence, Psacharopoulos and Hinchliffe (1972, pp. 786-792) conclude: "In manpower forecasting, the implicit assumption is that elasticity of substitution between one kind of labor and all other factors of production is zero. . . . At the other end of the scale, rate-of-return analysis implicitly assumes that the elasticity of substitution between any kind of labor and all other factors of production is infinite. Therefore, educational planning according to this approach should proceed on the basis of cost-benefit analysis since the actual numbers 'do not matter.' The implications of our findings in this context are that since high substitution possibilities do exist among the categories of educated labor examined, a rate-of-return framework is generally more justified than the manpower requirement approach."

Returns to education obtained by the individual have two parts: the extra, or differential, earnings associated with an increment of education (for example, the average additional pay that a college graduate receives over a high school graduate), and the psychic yields associated with such an increment (higher status, greater stability of employment, and more individual control over one's working conditions). The differences in earnings are intended to reflect extra pay expected over one's entire working lifetime. Because of compound interest, both returns and cost must be expressed in terms of their present discounted value. At first glance it might appear unwise to attribute all differential earnings to education itself and none to the possibility that persons who continue their education longer have greater natural abilities. This possibility becomes important when we try to assess the contribution of education to economic growth, but it is not relevant to the cost-benefit technique of education-

al planning. Other things being equal, a limitation in the number
of naturally talented persons, insofar as such a constraint on
performance is important, should simply speed up the process
of reaching equilibrium in the market for human services. The
private costs of education are measured as fees plus the net loss
of earnings attributable to being a student, minus student
grants. If a country wished to rely strictly on the market for
skills to regulate their production, then grants to students
would be reduced approximately to zero, and, furthermore, the
system would ensure that there is no differential burden on
income from labor as compared with earnings from physical
capital. Private returns might then be measured simply as differential earnings (excluding tax) plus psychic benefits, while costs
would be measured as fees plus foregone income.

Recognizing the social benefits of higher education, governments commonly subsidize students to some degree. To take
these public subsidies into account, education planners aim
toward equating marginal social benefits with marginal social
costs. Social benefits may then be computed as direct gains in
productivity attributable to extra education plus psychic benefits plus net external economies. Social costs are the sum of the
loss of a student's production in the marketplace while in
school plus the total of public subsidies toward tuition costs
(Layard, 1972).

Cost-benefit techniques would lead an educational planner to the following conclusions: If the lifetime earnings of, say,
medical doctors are high compared with the costs of medical
education, then the number of persons training to be doctors
should increase. But if the earnings of accountants are low compared with the cost of their professional education, then the
number of prospective accountants should be cut back. Cost-
benefit techniques specify the direction of change in educational supply; they do not specify how many more doctors or how
many fewer accountants should begin training. At least in theory, however, observation over time of the changes in returns
compared with costs should generate signals when the supply of
doctors has been sufficiently advanced and the supply of accountants reduced. For example, if the differential earnings of
doctors fail to equal the costs of medical education, school

administrators might then decide not to expand the size of their medical schools.

The cost-benefit approach to educational planning may seem to add nothing to the discussion earlier in this chapter about the automatic adjustment of university openings to market pressures, but this is not so. Cost-benefit analysis provides information to educational decision-makers quickly and assumes that they will respond to that information quickly by creating additional places in fields with shortages and cutting back in areas of surplus. It is a more positive, analytical attack on the problem than a simple reliance on decentralized signals from the market.

Though grounded on more realistic assumptions than is manpower requirements forecasting, cost-benefit techniques have their own peculiar shortcomings as procedures for educational planning. First, they gear supplies of different types of graduates to the free enterprise market—this, indeed, is their rationale. There is a question whether the market controls production for the ultimate benefit of the consumer, or whether the market itself is controlled by concentrations of economic power—for example, the two thousand largest corporations, which seek primarily to protect their own rates of growth, or, what amounts to the same thing, their survival (Galbraith, 1973). It is probably both unwise and unnecessary that a power elite dictates the choice of careers in our country.

A second and related point is that cost-benefit analysis does not offer guidance on the quality and type of training appropriate for service in sectors of the economy subject to administered salaries and wages, of which the public sector is the primary example. As our planet becomes more crowded, we require specialists to control the unwanted by-products of production. Naturally, private firms are more interested in turning out salable products than in dealing with their external diseconomies, so the protection of the environment becomes substantially a government responsibility. Because salaries and wages in public service are relatively rigid, we cannot expect cost-benefit analysis to provide clear signals for training future environmental specialists.

Third, cost-benefit estimates are necessarily based on data

that are, at best, drawn from the current operations of the economy. They are not predictions of what cost-benefit ratios will be in the future; if they were, we would be back in the world of manpower requirements projections. The production period of human skills is usually long, and colleges and universities face difficulties when they realize they should cut back on a particular training program, especially when the program is a . new one. Thus we can expect in any technologically progressive country that the mix of work skills specified by current cost-benefit ratios will be wrong if measured by the cost-benefit ratios prevailing when the newly trained labor enters the market. Incorrect signals remain incorrect even when one is able to show that a given type of labor can be easily substituted for other economic resources or vice versa. The market can make adjustments to errors in the supply of trained persons, but such errors are still made and are reflected in windfall gains and losses to different workers and a general loss in productivity.

Conclusions for Policy

Since the major forms of educational planning are flawed, we might conclude that any efforts to improve the economic efficiency of higher education are hopeless. This is not an altogether correct conclusion, but it is certainly true that, to be successful, such efforts require a broad base. We have been describing techniques of educational planning that are in use in some nonsocialist European countries and in parts of the developing world. More mathematically sophisticated models of planning, in which objective functions are precisely specified and in which economic and institutional constraints are dealt with explicitly, are also available. The character of the data, however, and the requirements of analysis in these optimizing models are such that they are not commonly used to establish policy guidelines (see Bowles, 1969; Adelman and Thorbecke, 1966, pp. 385-417).

Let us consider first the size of enrollments in undergraduate programs. Fairness in general and mobility for members of minority groups in particular are probably best achieved by having the maximum degree of openness. This conclusion rests on two points. First, undergraduate instruction is mainly general, and insofar as it is related to work it improves the general capacity of the student to learn and perform his eventual economic role, including economic roles within the household. Second, undergraduate education provides long-term yields to individuals in the form of consumption benefits that last through each person's lifetime—for example, a knowledge of language, history, political systems, and the arts. Furthermore, two conditions must be met in an open system of higher education. The first is that the system of finance of open enrollments itself must be equitable. The second is that study in higher education must reflect clearly the time preferences of students. If, for example, students want to pursue undergraduate study over a discontinuous period of time, they should suffer no disadvantage by doing so. Neither should students who wish to study in highly accelerated programs be penalized because access to first-line faculty is limited to full-time, strictly sequential four-year B.A. candidates.

Though the British have a somewhat more stratified system of education than we do, their government does not apply manpower planning techniques to the early stages of higher education. The White Paper on Education (Great Britain, Secretary of State for Education and Science, 1972, p. 31), noting that governments since 1963 have endorsed the general principle that higher education should be available for all those who are qualified and interested, and that their subsequent career patterns must be expected to differ significantly from those of their predecessors, observed that the expansion of higher education had already reached the point where employers' requirements for such highly qualified people were largely being met.

> Opportunities for higher education are not
> ... to be determined primarily by reference to
> broad estimates of the country's future need for
> highly qualified people, although attempts to relate
> supply to demand in certain specialized profes-
> sions—and, particularly, at the postgraduate stage—

will be no less important than before. The government considers higher education valuable for its
contribution to the personal development of those
who pursue it; at the same time they value its continued expansion as an investment in the nation's
human talent in a time of rapid social change and
technological development.

Closer to home, one may note that a similar position was
taken in early 1973 by the New York State Task Force on
Financing Higher Education. In its report to Governor Nelson
A. Rockefeller, the task force offered as its first recommenda-
tion that "every New York State high school graduate with the
desire and ability to pursue postsecondary education should be
provided full opportunity to do so without regard to financial
ability, sex, race, or geographic residence in the state" (p. 1).
Enrollment in undergraduate programs should thus be respon-
sive exclusively to the social demand for admission. Social demand, being functionally related to household income, parents'
education, quality of elementary and secondary school programs, and student subsidies, is amenable to study and prediction (Hoenack, 1968).

Beyond undergraduate education, regulation of the supply of persons for standard categories should be left to the
operation of the market. As we have seen, this is not a perfect
solution to the problem of maintaining economic efficiency in
higher education. But given the inadequacies of manpower planning in a technologically active society and the political difficulties of attempting to regulate the number of students in post-
graduate education, it seems to be the preferred procedure.

However, the government should take special interest in
some occupations and assignments, and for these positive manpower planning is urgently needed. The 1971 Annual Report of
the President's Council of Economic Advisers speaks in some
detail of natural priorities and claims upon the national product (pp. 92-93). But, more important, we must free national
economic policy from its obsession with growth in GNP, with
the balance of payments, and with control of inflation (not that
such matters are unimportant, but they have become ends in

themselves rather than means to economic well-being), and speak instead of consumption goals and the quality of life. This process would begin with estimating the minimum requirements per household for housing, nutrition, health care, education, recreation, and transportation; it would extend to ensuring opportunities for individual expression and artistic creation; and it would seek to provide these services and opportunities under conditions in which environmental quality would be improved. As Mahbub ul Hag, former chief economist of the government of Pakistan, has said (1972, p. 98), "Let us worry about the *content* of GNP, even more than its rate of increase." The second step would be to translate material objectives about consumption standards and the quality of life into estimates of societal needs for persons with special skills, over and beyond what the private sector might be expected to employ. The third step would be for the government to see that appropriate numbers of places in institutions were available for the training of these specialists. The fourth and presumably final step would be for the government to see that the specialists were properly engaged, in either the private or the public sector, in tasks that contributed to the fulfillment of social objectives.

Weathersby (1972, pp. 30-31) describes the matter as follows:

> There seems little argument that there is currently a surplus of scientific and professional manpower who are either underemployed or unemployed. . . . If we would just speed up the economy, possibly through tax cuts, investment credit, and deficit spending, increase space expenditures by, for example, initiating a new multibillion dollar space shuttle project, and even increase federal support for research and development and education—then our scientific manpower problems would be over and all would be well again. Or would they? . . . Instead of beginning with the symptoms of excess supply and asking "what went wrong?", we think it would be very fruitful to begin by asking, "Where do we want the United States to be in five years? How would we know if we got there?" In other words, to begin with even a crude and impre-

cise statement of national objectives from which
we deduce objectives for intermediate goals such as
manpower. Only in this way can we hold a measuring rod up against the problem and judge its actual
size.

According to this argument, attainment of economic efficiency
in higher education, efficiency that may serve social objectives,
is primarily a problem for government, not for colleges and
universities themselves, to solve.

Finally, the economic efficiency of higher education can
be increased when institutions make use of those manpower
projections that can be presumed to be reasonably accurate. We
have noted how predictable the teacher surplus was and how we
lost valuable opportunities by failing to recognize its existence
in time. Similarly, it would be easy to predict the requirements
for, say, health personnel by making assumptions about the
effects of labor-labor and labor-capital substitutions, such as
group practice and changes in capital-based medical technology.
To effectively use these projections in large, stable, socially important fields of employment, colleges and universities must be
willing to cut back programs as well as expand them. They must
also be willing to explain such actions to the public and to
actively publicize their predictions of both the supply and the
costs of future high-level manpower.

2

Allocating Scarce Resources

Whereas the criterion of economic efficiency demands that an economic activity turn out the appropriate quantity, quality, and types of products, the criterion of technological efficiency demands that these products are produced with a minimum of waste. Imagine that a university system is graduating more engineers than can find work while numerous vacancies exist in architecture. Ignoring for the moment workers' preferences (people may derive more satisfaction from being engineers than from being architects, even if employment prospects favor the latter), and accepting the market mechanisms as a means to reveal consumers' preferences for different types of trained manpower, we can conclude that economic efficiency will be increased if undergraduates are directed away from engineering courses and toward architectural courses, whether through advertising, counseling or peer pressure. The benefit of having one more architect outweighs the loss of having one fewer engineer.

Technological efficiency is measured differently. Suppose there are two engineering schools in an area, each of which enrolls students of roughly equal aptitude and graduates engineers of roughly equal proficiency (measured, possibly, by their successful advancement once hired). Suppose further that one school spends twice as much money per student as the other. The high-spending school might be called wasteful, or technologically inefficient. The first principle of economics is the scarcity of resources—somewhere in the world somebody needs more goods and services than existing resources can provide. The second principle is that resources have alternative uses.

Hence, waste represents lost opportunities for supplying ourselves with more needed goods and services.

Introduction

In the late 1960s, it was thought possible to apply planning-programing-budgeting systems (PPBS) techniques to higher education (Keller, 1970). If that had been true or if it becomes true in the future, questions of technological efficiency could be rigorously analyzed. But the requirements of this kind of analysis are very large. First, PPBS requires defining institutional objectives operationally. This is extraordinarily difficult to do for research outputs. For instruction, one can speak of enrollments, graduates, and so on, but true objectives embrace the quality of the end results—for example, whether graduates in English are able to study literature more sensitively and perceptively than graduates of five years ago. Such measurement is largely subjective and does not fit well with mathematical models of college and university planning. Second, PPBS requires the capacity to compare the cost-effectiveness of alternate means of accomplishing objectives, to decide whether one approach takes the institution further toward accomplishing the stated objective for any expenditure than does another. To make these comparisons the analyst must thoroughly understand educational production relationships. Take instruction in economics, for example. What combination of large lectures, seminars, and laboratory work is more effective in teaching honor students in econometrics? Or average students in the economics of development? To what degree is the effectiveness of large lectures enhanced by the use of television or films? To what extent are economics and computer science complementary? Unfortunately, answers to such questions are not easy to find.

Certain more limited kinds of analysis are possible using PPBS (Rivlin, 1969). Program accounting—for example, establishing the amounts and kinds of resources committed to various instructional and research programs within the university— helps illuminate decisions about future commitments (Romney, 1971; Ziemer, Young, and Tapping, 1971).

The first Newman report on higher education (U.S. Department of Health, Education and Welfare, 1971, p. 31) concluded that analysis should be microeconomic, that is, focused on the cost and outputs of particular departments and programs. The report "that it is within individual departments and educational programs that cost-effectiveness thinking will be most rewarding. . . . That is where its payoff is—in making it less costly for students to learn English, or political science, or electrical engineering. . . . The professor needs to ask whether his lectures actually teach as much as the same amount of time spent guiding the independent reading of his students, whether some kind of practicum would help them to grasp better the interrelations of different parts of the subject matter." The Newman task force also took the position that neither the absence of well-grounded theories of learning nor the inability to cast the analysis in, say, econometric terms, stands in the way of obtaining useful results. It said that "precise analysis is not necessary in order to make significant improvements. . . . At several universities . . . large differences in cost of teaching an undergraduate in roughly comparable departments exist, differences as great as two or even three to one. . . . While measuring the effective learning in each situation can only be done in an approximate way, to ignore the possibility of improving cost effectiveness inherent in such figures seems irresponsible."

An apparently successful example of the analysis described by the Newman task force is that of Breneman (1970), who in his studies of graduate education at the University of California, Berkeley, was able to show that, measured in student man-years, the cost of obtaining the Ph.D. varied widely among departments—it was low, for example, in chemistry, and high in French literature. Breneman demonstrated that the differences in costs could not be attributed only to the fact that students in science are more likely to obtain fellowships and other aid than students studying languages. In his analysis, the difference in costs was related to peculiarities of the faculty incentive structure within the different departments. Earlier, Thorstein Veblen (1918) offered an analysis of such incentives in higher education. Though one should not necessarily draw a causal relation between such studies as Breneman's and university policy, Berkeley now operates under a set of productivity quotas, with graduate departments receiving rewards for the speed and regularity with which they produce degree-holders.

One may, of course, take a broader view of technological efficiency in higher education. Hettich (1971) has indicated that productivity in a group of forty-nine Canadian universities and colleges declined from 1956-1957 to 1967-1968, the last year of his study. According to Hettich, the chief reason for the decline was increases in the foregone income of students, the costs of which increase as the average number of student years per degree go up. From 1962-1963 to 1967-1968, productivity declined in terms of faculty input as well. The output measure used by Hettich was the number of degrees and diplomas awarded, weighted by the average starting salaries degree and diploma holders. His study was focused on instructional inputs and outputs, not on research activity.

Let us now distinguish between direct and induced productivity change. In colleges and universities, direct productivity changes might occur when students lengthened or shortened the time they needed to earn various degrees and certificates, which could happen if degree requirements were altered. Productivity changes would also occur if faculties took action to reduce their workloads by reducing the number of classes taught. There is some evidence that faculty in large private universities have succeeded in doing so. The number of fulltime faculty per 100 full-time students rose from 9.6 in 1953-1954 to 11.8 in 1966-1967 (O'Neill, 1971).

Induced productivity change takes place when colleges and universities are affected by productivity developments outside the educational sector. In general, productivity changes are more likely to occur outside the educational sector than within, even though one of the sources of advances in productivity is the university's contribution to new knowledge. Baumol writes (1967, p. 57) that if productivity per man-hour rises progressively in one sector of the economy compared to its rate of growth elsewhere in the economy, while wages rise steadily in all sectors, then costs in the nonprogressive sectors will inevitably increase, cumulatively and without limit. "For while in the progressive sector productivity increases will serve as an offset to rising wages," he says "this offset must be smaller in the nonprogressive sector. . . . Thus, the very progress of the technologically progressive sector inevitably adds to the costs of the technologically unchanging sectors of the economy, unless somehow the labor markets in these areas can be sealed off and wages held absolutely constant, a most unlikely possibility." With respect to education, Baumol suggests that, "as productivity in the remainder of the economy continues to increase, costs of running the educational organizations will mount correspondingly, so that whatever the magnitudes of the funds they need today, we can be reasonably certain that they will require more tomorrow, and even more on the day after that."

The outlook, then, may be for continuing declines in the technological efficiency of higher education, compared to more progressive industries. But it is possible to take the opposite view. Financial pressures on institutions are stimulating investigations of how better to use faculty time (Bowen and Douglass, 1971). Advanced placement of students and early admissions reduce the time required for students to earn the B.A., yielding savings to the student and to his college or university as well. The substitution of machines—language laboratories, television, and computers—for faculty is being seriously discussed.

Another development that will undoubtedly affect technological efficiency is the unionization of faculty. Faculty in public institutions are under considerable pressure to engage in collective bargaining because other public employees are rapidly becoming unionized. Unless faculty are represented and obtain written contracts, they will lose benefits to other, more tightly organized groups. In private institutions similar pressure exists when nonteaching staff become organized. At first glance it might seem that unionization would reduce technological efficiency, but we shall argue later that it will instead cause faculty to give greater time and emphasis to their teaching responsibilities and thus heighten productivity.

Planning-Programing-Budgeting Systems

In 1959 Kershaw and McKean maintained that the time
was approaching when it would be possible to make quantitative comparisons of educational systems:

> By "system" we mean a set of interrelated
> factors that are used together to produce an out-
> put. Thus an air force is a system; so is a public
> school system, a university, a business corporation.
> All of these systems produce some sort of output.
> ... These systems also have costs associated with
> them, costs which may be expressed in dollars or in
> labor of certain specified skills or in lives lost or in
> smog produced and so on .... Finally, in all of
> these systems there are various ways of combining
> the elements or inputs in order to produce results.
> This is what makes the system interesting from an
> analytical point of view; it is possible to vary its
> inputs and see what the effect is on output. ...
> The purpose of comparing one system with anoth-
> er is to show which is better, or, more frequently,
> since quantitative analysis can rarely embrace all
> considerations, the purpose is to compare systems
> in a way that is relevant to a choice between them
> and *helps* one to decide which is better [pp. 1-2].

In a similar vein, Deitch (1960) suggested that university
administrators should make use of "marginal return calculations" in deciding how to allocate resources for the achievement
of specific objectives. He maintained that administrators should
provide themselves with three major kinds of information: the
objectives of the institution and the relative importance of each;
the variables the administrator can control and those which he
cannot; and the relationships between controllable variables and
achievement of important objectives. With such knowledge at
hand, administrators could relate returns from different variables to each dollar of expenditure and reach an equilibrium
that maximized output in the allocation of institutional resources.

Planning-programing-budgeting systems (PPBS) originated

in a special part of the public sector—the military. Through conscious scrutiny, PPBS was intended to apply the evaluation methods of the marketplace to defense problems. In the marketplace, consumer acceptance measures the relative worth of the outputs of a business firm. In the marketplace, the engineer gives information to management about the least costly methods of producing given products. Unless a firm makes products that people want, and unless it makes a good choice of input mix (on grounds of cost and technological efficiency), it cannot survive.

By applying these evaluation methods to defense, the following elements of economic decision-making were established (Hitch and McKean, 1961, pp. 118-120): choice of objectives (what aim or aims is one trying to accomplish?); examination of alternatives by which the objective may be accomplished; determination of resource costs associated with each alternative procedure; preparation of a *model*—or means of analysis—to relate the degrees by which objectives are achieved to increments of costs; and specification of criteria for choosing among alternative procedures (ordinarily these criteria would be benefit-cost ratios—one would choose the alternative yielding the highest ratio—but when there are multiple objectives described in terms that cannot be compared, the criteria would be approximations of benefit-cost ratios).

Even though the military never succeeded in establishing an operational definition of an ultimate objective, such as "military worth" or "deterrence of war," PPBS had become a well-accepted process of general analysis in the Defense Department by the early 1960s. On the assumption that whatever worked in the Defense Department could be applied elsewhere, President Lyndon Johnson announced in 1965 that PPBS would be implemented throughout the federal government. This action was surely the high point of enthusiasm for scientific analysis of resource distribution processes in the public sector.

Translated into the context of domestic social programs, the PPBS process embraces the following goals: "careful identification and examination of goals and objectives in each major area of activity; analysis of "the *output* of a given program in terms of its objectives"; "measurement of total program costs, not for just one year but for at least several years ahead"; "formulation of objectives and programs extending beyond the single year of the annual budget submission"; and "analysis of alternatives to find the most effective means of reaching basic program objectives and to achieve these objectives for the least cost" (Schultze, 1968, p. 19).

Presented in such outline, PPBS appears to be rational in the extreme. One may only wonder why governments prepare budgets in any other way. Yet most governments operate on a very different basis. For both economic and political reasons, government budget officers, as well as service chiefs, customarily avoid precise specification of goals and objectives.

The economic reason for this behavior is that the outputs of public agencies are commonly many and disparate; their yield frequently is measurable only after a considerable lapse of time, if at all. Consequently, stating objectives with any degree of precision requires value judgments about the worth of different outputs at any particular moment.

There are also political explanations for current budgeting procedures. First, stating objectives stirs up controversy among persons who hold different views about what a particular agency should be doing. Second, revealing one's goals invites accountability for results, and because it is generally difficult to measure output, concern for accountability may shift the focus of an agency toward those activities that are most easily subject to quantitative assessment. Moreover, budgets are commonly prepared on an incremental basis. "Because political decision costs tend to mount the more the decisions conflict with values held by important groups and because our ability to foresee the full social consequences of any program change is so limited, movement toward objectives should proceed by small steps . . . correcting for unforeseen consequences as we go" (Schultze, 1968, pp. 49-50).

The enthusiasm of the federal government for PPBS was remarkably short-lived. This sharp reversal of attitude at the federal level dampened efforts to apply PPBS to such institutions as colleges and universities (although, as we shall see, colleges and universities have their own special problems in using PPBS). Federal government departments are no longer required to prepare annual budget requests in PPBS form. In papers prepared for the Joint Economic Committee of the U. S. Congress (1969), PPBS was characterized as a "Rube Goldberg apparatus" and a "fatal triumph of financial management over economics."

What went wrong? It seems clear that PPBS was vastly oversold on three counts. First, some early advocates implied that PPBS could guide both broad and narrow allocations of resources in the public sector. But in general PPBS offers no means for weighing the importance of different major objectives. Once objectives are stated and broad allocations of resources are decided upon, however, PPBS is a logical process in some instances for choosing among various means. William Gorham, a leading advocate of PPBS, offered the following statement to Congress (U.S. Congress, Joint Economic Committee, 1967, p. 5): "We have not attempted any grandiose cost-benefit analysis designed to reveal whether the total benefits from an additional million dollars spent on health programs would be higher or lower than that from an additional million spent on education or welfare. If I was ever naive enough to think this sort of analysis possible, I no longer am."

Second, almost all advocates of PPBS argue that the system should be adopted on a large scale, not selectively or experimentally. Yet the difficulty in making quantitative estimates of inputs and outputs in public programs varies enormously even within one enterprise. Making such estimates is even more difficult when one compares different enterprises— for example, it is difficult to estimate inputs and outputs in the health sciences, but easy in highway development. The competence of budget staffs to carry out involved PPBS exercises also varies widely among different departments. Introduction of PPBS forced civil servants to do what they knew they could not do well; thus, they understandably viewed PPBS with cynicism and mockery. Because of these factors, PPBS could never be implemented on a broad scale—and piecemeal implementation was never very successful.

Third, the opportunities for high-grade policy analysis, a crucial aim of PPBS, are markedly different from one agency to the next. Not only are some problems of resource distribution more amenable to cost-effectiveness analysis than others, but the confluence of a talented group of analysts in an agency at the moment when a suitable problem appears is a more or less random event. The belief that all budget offices in the federal government were able to develop cost-effectiveness analysis of alternative means of carrying forward a program was clearly mistaken.

Two other difficulties are worth noting. First, PPBS assumes a flexibility that is frequently not present in public bureaucracies. When the acceptance of PPBS necessitates some radical changes in the methods of providing a service, those whose status or jobs are threatened can be expected to thwart the shift, even while proclaiming the worth of the new ideas. Such persons can use various means to prevent change in public service; assigning work according to seniority is the most easily noted, but there are certainly others.

Second, PPBS assumes the acquiescence of public interest groups affected by major changes in the provision of services. Once a group has become accustomed to being taken care of by the operation of any program, it rarely wants to yield its favored position to increase the technological efficiency of the service for the whole population. Affected public interest groups are likely to use political influence to see that some changes recommended by advocates of PPBS are not implemented.

As public or quasi-public institutions, colleges and universities are faced with many obstacles to the full-fledged adoption of PPBS. Consider the difficulty faced by administrators in determining allocations to major functions—the functions of instruction, pure research, applied research, community service, for example. PPBS does not offer guidance on the relative values of humanitarian and scientific learning unless one takes the approach that university allocations should be directed by the difference in earnings of arts graduates and science graduates. This is the cost-benefit approach we discussed and rejected in the last chapter. But even this approach would not give clear signals about the degree to which science majors should take courses in art, history, language, or music, nor the extent to which arts students should develop some understanding of the methods of scientific inquiry. Moreover, PPBS does not help determine the proper division in institutional budgets between research and instruction. "That basic research and graduate training and the provision of undergraduate educational services are carried on within the same institutions and frequently by the same individuals . . . suggests that the two activities are complementary in production in the sense that fewer scarce resources are needed to produce given amounts of the two goods if they are produced together rather than separately" (Nerlove, 1972, p. S209). The same facility—a laboratory or computer center, for example—may be used for both instruction and research, so that the cost of physical capital is shared by the two functions. Further, the existence of strong research programs may attract highly motivated graduate students who reinforce each other's academic drives and who are available for teaching of lower division students, allowing a greater degree of specialization in instruction.

Colleges and universities, as we have said, do not easily make quantitative assessments of their inputs and outputs. Outputs, for example, may be measured by degrees awarded to students and by patents claimed by researchers. In both instruction and research, however, the number of people finishing any program of study or investigation is not as important as the thoroughness with which skills have been imparted and the usefulness of inventions, and results frequently cannot be detected for decades. The time lag in judging such changes make PPBS methods ineffective in controlling year-to-year shifts in resource allocations.

Likewise, preparation of cost-effectiveness studies in higher education is difficult. General problems of measuring inputs and outputs abound. In addition, many highly effective learning processes depend upon a special interaction between professor and student that raises the motivation and interest of each. This interaction is not easily subject to measurement, nor can one predict the response of faculty member to student and vice versa any more readily than one can say that a given painting or musical score will appeal to a particular individual. Indeed, the response of the individual, either faculty member or student, depends on his set of intellectual experiences. Methods for assessing that unique record of growth, in order to obtain a better match between faculty members and students, are not very well developed. Such intellectual matching might be compared with computer dating—efficient but dull. Illusive interpersonal reactions distort the information one needs about the relative effectiveness of lectures, seminars, and individualized study as modes of instruction.

Academic institutions are subject as well to bureaucratic rigidities. Analysis might indicate that central libraries are more efficient than departmental facilities, but senior faculty may prefer the latter and may have sufficient political power to keep them. To improve delivery of their lectures, faculty may be asked to allow themselves to be videotaped and to receive criticism on the taped material. But they also may simply refuse to accept this analysis of their work.

Colleges and universities seldom make radical proposals to change the services they offer except in response to the pressures of an aroused public. For example, a prestigious private university might decide that it would be to its advantage to concentrate its resources on locating youth of unusual intellectual competence from all income classes. This policy would antagonize alumni who wished to enroll their sons and daughters in the institution and who might then threaten to withdraw their financial support. Expecting such a response, university officials would delay the change in policy until public demand for improved distribution of educational opportunities was strong. In another instance, a community college faculty might want to increase the political awareness of its students, but the residents of the city or town in which the college was located might become enraged by the resulting student demonstrations. The change would occur only if the general public demanded that educational institutions seek to develop the political consciousness of their students.

Balderston and Weathersby (1972, p. 51) offer this summary of the use of PPBS in higher education:

> Educational institutions foster diversity, seek differentiated instead of homogenous viewpoints, operate on a collegial system in which each faculty member considers himself *primus inter pares,* decentralize management to dozens of department chairmen and deans, and rarely attempt to determine institutionwide operational objectives. In higher education the informal collegial structure is often more important than the formal structure of rotating department chairmen and transient presidents. Without clearly defined objectives and without sharp lines of authority and responsibility, the formal structure of PPBS serves little use beyond giving outsiders a false sense of precision and security. While basic analysis is often very useful for educational decision-making, . . . the organizational and political environment of most institutions of higher education effectively precludes the full implementation of PPBS.

Has the noble effort to develop a scientific basis for resource allocation in higher education had any positive effect? PPBS has clearly been helpful in some ways, even though no broad-based set of operational principles has appeared. We now discuss some of these positive legacies.

Program Accounting. Financial accounts may be arranged to show expenditures by function—how much is spent, for example, to provide instruction in first-year mathematics or how much is spent on counseling services for various types of students. This practice is called *program accounting.* It allows the administration and, indeed, all parties to make comparisons over time. For example, without program accounting, it might not be apparent that the relative share of institutional resources spent on the operation of the central library had been declining. This fact alone does not establish a basis for increasing the library budget, but it does make it reasonable to ask whether an unexpanding central library can supply services to a growing campus. Program accounting allows interested persons to monitor the results of intrauniversity struggles for budgetary resources and come to the aid of those who, for whatever reason, have had their legitimate claims ignored.

Program accounting also allows administrators and others to compare the functional uses of resources in different campuses, institutions, and departments. Again, the information simply provides a basis for raising questions about whether existing distributions make sense or whether changes should be considered.

The National Center for Higher Education Management Systems at the Western Interstate Commission for Higher Education (1971) has done pioneer work in establishing model program accounts. The accounting systems they have devised delineate the major functions to which resources may be allocated—instruction, research, public service, and so forth—and allow proration of instructional costs to departments on a unit basis. Fixed instructional costs are distinguished from variable costs, and accounting procedures are laid out to facilitate the projection of costs under alternative assumptions about future enrollments, faculty size, pay scales, and so on.

Simulation Models. College and university administrators are constantly seeking answers to hypothetical questions. What if the proportion of instruction of lower division students carried out by senior faculty were increased by 25 percent? What if the proportion of juniors becoming science majors were to double over the next five years? What if instructional television were used instead of large lectures? Simulation models allow universities and colleges to explore the cost implications of these questions under a variety of assumptions, taking into account the many complexities and interrelationships in institutions (Judy, 1972).

The procedure in preparing a simulation model is to compute ratios between numbers of students in the different college and university programs—undergraduate, graduate school, professional school, and so on—and numbers of faculty. Likewise one computes ratios between students and required library resources, laboratory stations, dormitory and eating facilities, and the like. A computer program is written to allow one to make forecasts of resource commitments required (or released) under various assumed changes in enrollments. The coefficients which serve to translate changes in enrollments into changes in required resources are generally based initially on observed, historical data, but they can easily be established as policy parameters. For example, it might be determined as a matter of university policy to increase student-faculty ratios in the humanities and at the same time to reduce them in the sciences. In the ordinary case, such a policy shift would be implemented gradually, not immediately. The simulation model would recognize a gradual reduction in the ratio relating student enrollments to faculty in the humanities and a gradual increase in the sciences. Results obtained from the computer would allow one to trace these forecast changes in faculty composition over the relevant period of time.

Policy Analysis. PPBS incorporates policy analysis directly into the budgetary process. Although policy analysis existed long before PPBS came onto the scene, one lasting result of the interest in PPBS, though now a largely deflated one, is that policy analysis has become much more widely appreciated and practiced even when it is not directly linked to the budget-making process.

Policy analysis may be used to determine whether and under what conditions of enrollment and class size year-round operation of a given campus is cost-effective. It may indicate the likelihood of interdepartmental spillovers (Balderston and Weathersby, 1972). For example, will the performance of economics majors, who need to be able to use mathematics, improve when the mathematics department raises the quality of instruction it offers in lower division courses?

Measurement problems abound, and we are a long way from knowing when a dollar subtracted from the budget of any department would produce an identical reduction of "goodness." As the first Newman Report (U.S. Department of Health, Education and Welfare, Office of Education, 1971) indicated, however, common-sense policy analysis can help a great deal when studying departmental activities. One useful exercise is to examine at the departmental level the incentive structures under which faculty work. (Later in this chapter, we draw attention to an especially provocative study of this kind—and to the policy changes it led to.) However, when administrators make efforts to change the incentives that guide faculty actions, they must recognize that organized faculty will take their own positions with respect to the manipulation of the incentive structure. This relatively new development, the rise of collective bargaining in higher education, is the topic to which we now turn.

Collective Bargaining

Collective bargaining is on the rise in higher education. Faculty members, as well as secretarial staff members, maintenance workers, and others, are organizing on an unprecedented scale. On-going unions in elementary and secondary schools provide ready-made leadership. Moreover, since collective bargaining is highly developed in state government, public university employees are pressured to organize simply as a defensive strategy. Similarly, the organization of nonteaching employees in private universities puts pressure on faculty members in those institutions to unionize. As Howe states (1972, p. 2), "The State University of New York, the state college systems of New Jersey and Pennsylvania, the City University of New York, Rutgers, Central Michigan, Oakland, and more recently Rhode Island, along with other institutions equally worthy of mention, represent a substantial bridgehead to the ranks of four-year colleges and universities."

As of spring 1973, 314 institutions were engaged in collective bargaining by faculty units; 120 of these were four-year colleges or universities. Although a majority (194) were two-year community colleges they were responsible only for 19,260 faculty members, while the four-year group now numbers 52,115 faculty. (The large number of faculty in the CUNY system must be considered here.) Most of these units are contained in eight states: New York (84), Michigan (32), Pennsylvania (27), New Jersey (25), Washington (24), Wisconsin (23), Illinois (21), and Minnesota (18). (See Aussieker and Garbarino, 1973, and Hodgkinson, 1973.)

Although there has been competition between the National Education Association (NEA), responsible for the largest number of bargaining units, and the American Federation of Teachers (AFT) it is interesting to note the merger of the New York State Teachers Association (NEA) and the United Teachers of New York (AFT). The elimination of this competition may mean even more power and acceptance for unionism among faculty of four-year colleges and universities.

Higher education is vulnerable to collective bargaining for three reasons: First, as we have just seen, a systematic, scientific, and unified method of controlling resource allocations in higher education is unavailable; faculty are therefore free to define personnel benefits (higher salaries, lower workloads, and so on) as improvements in quality of education. Second, education is highly labor intensive; that is, the prospects for offsetting faculty benefits by increases in productivity—the substitution, say, of capital for labor—have been viewed up to now as remote. Third, for the equitable distribution of educational opportunities and the securing of the social benefits of higher education, student fees are commonly set below the full cost of instruction; hence faculty and other university employees find themselves protected from the market restraints imposed on unions operating in the profit-making sector of the economy. While a union in the private sector would not willingly force an employer into bankruptcy by unreasonable demands, a state university system, operating as a monopolistic supplier of educational services to large groups of state residents, is not subject to the full measure of market forces that employees in private firms often feel (Doherty, 1972, p. 3).

The pressure for unionization has been increased by presidential executive orders (such as President Nixon's Executive Order 11491, October 29, 1969) specifying that federal employees have the right to form and join labor organizations. Following such initiatives the American Federation of State, County, and Municipal Employees has successfully lobbied for the introduction of a bill in Congress to create a National Public Employees Relations Act, which would extend to nonfederal public employees the rights of collective bargaining enjoyed by workers in the private sector. Several states, notably New York and Michigan, now extend such rights to faculty in public institutions.

Let us consider the possible effects of the unionization of faculty at the apex of our academic structure, the large prestige university, an institution that offers instruction to undergraduates and graduate students in scientific, humanistic, and professional fields and that is responsible for the creation of new knowledge through research. We concentrate on this institution because it can greatly influence other institutions in the educational system and because unionization will produce more profound changes in the major university than in state and community colleges (see Benson, 1972; Duryea and Fisk, 1973, give a more complete treatment of faculty unionization in different institutions).

What results can be expected from the unionization of university faculty? Collective bargaining is likely to bring about a remarkable change in the power alignments within universities, even though such alignments between universities and the outside world remain approximately the same. In major universities, the faculty now holds a great deal of power; indeed, faculty are at the same time employees and employers, especially those who move into and out of administrative positions—department heads, deans, provosts, and so forth. But by custom respected professors who are not at all involved in management positions are also consulted about departmental appointments and major policy developments. Not all faculty hold a place in the inner circle of power; young teachers are excluded, though seniority alone does not assure a place. Great accomplishment in research and writing opens the door to power; success in obtaining grants and service on university committees may also. But the rules are flexible and not easily quantified. Counting pages is one way to judge research output, but one article that represents a breakthrough—and only those who hold power are entitled to decide what is a breakthrough—is worth a dozen published in third- or fourth-rate journals.

Collective bargaining offers little to university faculty already in the inner circle of power; in fact, it is likely to cause them to lose power. The push for collective bargaining in higher education will probably come from faculty members who regard themselves as outsiders—younger people and those the present system does not favor, such as faculty members interested primarily in teaching or public service rather than in basic ("pure") research. Collective bargaining is a means for those outside the formal and informal power structures of universities to gain power for themselves.

Two groups of outsiders are readily identifiable in large institutions: younger faculty members and those senior faculty members who disapprove of the almost exclusive use of research skills and contributions as the measure of professional excellence. Since those senior faculty members accuse the present system of harming students (the highly successful faculty member is frequently too busy with research to meet individually with students and, so it is alleged, may spend too little time on his teaching duties), and since younger faculty sympathize with students anyway, these two groups of outsiders may well be natural allies in their concern with student welfare.

Once this new power alignment wins a university representation election and, as in New York, New Jersey, Michigan, Massachusetts, and Wisconsin, no serious legal barrier stands in the way of collective bargaining in higher education, what is likely to follow? The easy answer is that faculty will bargain hard for salary increases and, to a lesser degree, for decreases in workload. But if these are the only changes collective bargaining brings about, then it would have little effect on higher education in America. This is not to say that there would be no effect at all. Certainly, higher education would become more expensive. Part of the rising costs would probably be passed along to students and their families, even though considerations of fairness might dictate otherwise. Perhaps more students would attend state colleges and universities instead of more expensive private universities, and perhaps for some students informal education would replace formal studies. Therefore, though demand for education in general may not be greatly influenced by price considerations, demand for those forms of higher education that are especially vulnerable to faculty unionization may be strongly influenced.

Claims by faculty for higher pay and smaller classes, however, may simply conceal a more profound struggle over changing the way universities are run. Traditionally, collective bargaining aims toward the equal treatment of employees—indeed, one of the prime forces leading to the introduction of bargaining is the feeling that management has treated employees unequally, favoring those who support the system and being antagonistic to those who speak out against it. As Supreme Court Justice Jackson said in 1944, "The practice and philosophy of collective bargaining looks with suspicion upon individual advantage. . . . The workman is free, if he values his own bargaining position more than that of the group, to vote against representation; but the majority rules, and if it collectivizes the employment bargain, individual advantages of favor will generally in practice go in as a contribution to the collective result" (quoted in Wollett, 1971, pp. 18-19).

No one proposes that all faculty be treated exactly alike at all times—all faculty need not receive the same pay, for example. But making inequality tolerable under majority rule requires precision. Grievance machinery must be set up so that contracts can be enforced and opposing parties can be legally represented in grievance procedures. Article XVI of the Collective Bargaining Agreement between the Association of Pennsylvania State College and University Faculties/Pennsylvania Association for Higher Education (APSCUF/PAHE) and the Commonwealth of Pennsylvania provides criteria and procedure for promotions: "An individual faculty member shall have the right to grieve . . . promotion decisions only as to himself and then only with respect to failure to observe the procedures set forth . . . or insofar as other provisions of this agreement may have been violated."

This provision might seem to rule out invidious comparisons, such as one professor demanding to be promoted on the grounds that his research and teaching are at least the equal of those of another professor who has recently received advancement. But since merit is a matter of judgment, comparisons are certain to be made. The most relevant comparisons are those among fellow faculty members within an institution. If there is general dissatisfaction with the way promotions are being handled, the union itself may grieve. The article provides that "APSCUF/PAHE shall have the right to grieve . . . with regard to substantial changes in the pattern of granting promotions." If rules are to be understood by third parties, they must be expressed in quantitative terms. But we have already indicated that research productivity is not quantifiable, and its assessment is largely judgmental. Thus it cannot be a judicially determined basis for advancement. Imagine that Professor X believes he has been passed over for promotion in favor of Professor Y. Professor X's lawyer could call expert witnesses to state that his client's book is at least as good as that of Professor Y, and the university lawyer could likewise call expert witnesses to contend that Professor X's book lacks merit while Y's book is outstanding. But it would be a messy and ego-bruising process. According to academic tradition, what can be done quietly in a committee room cannot be done well in public, even though in countries such as Norway, faculty, wearing formal dress, are examined by their peers in public meetings.

What happens to seniority as a means of regulating advancement? Seniority is the most common advancement mechanism dealt with in union contracts. Experience in public sector bargaining shows that while seniority may come to play a marginally greater role than it does now, it will not replace research productivity as the prime criterion for advancement. Two reasons are that faculty members favor merit as the basis for promotion and that younger faculty, who are most likely to support collective bargaining, cannot accept a system based exclusively on seniority.

However, teaching proficiency will probably replace research productivity as the chief criterion for judging merit, at least in large universities. The purpose of teaching is better understood by most people than the purpose of research. In addition, to be judged on the basis of teaching is less threatening to most faculty members than to be judged on the basis of research output. If one's teaching is deficient, then hard work can improve it; but a person may have no confidence about his ability to upgrade his or her analysis and writing. Collective bargaining may thus bring the comfort long sought by many university faculty. Most important, in a number of nonthreatening ways, the assessment of teaching proficiency is quantifiable. A teacher can submit information on class hours, number of courses taught, new courses introduced, textbooks written, questionnaires submitted to students, filmstrips prepared, class enrollments, and graduates. Of course, if one goes on to measure how much students have learned in Professor X's classes, then assessment may once again become threatening.

Two major contracts support the contention that teaching proficiency will rise in importance in the awarding of promotions. The Pennsylvania contract mentioned above lists, in order, the following criteria of promotion: effective teaching, fulfillment of professional responsibilities, mastery of subject matter in the discipline, contribution to the college, and continuing scholarly growth (Article XVI, A.2). Similarly, the contract between the Board of Higher Education of the City of New York and the Legislative Conference (City University of New York), 1969-1972, provided in Article XVII that the evaluation of professional competence would give attention to such elements as classroom instruction and related activities; administrative assignments; research; scholarly writing; departmental, college, and university committee assignments; and student counseling. The article goes on to establish a basis for a one-hour observation of the faculty member's work, for an annual consultation with the department chairman, and for written evaluations of the faculty member's work to be prepared by the department chairman. The department chairman is likely to be in a better position to make judgments about teaching, counseling, committee assignments, and so forth, than about highly specialized research, especially when that research falls outside his particular field of interest. Thus the procedure itself minimizes the significance of research in promotion.

Would this shift in criteria underlying faculty advancement affect the productivity of universities? Consider the following: first, faculty would become more willing to spend time in teaching, including the teaching of undergraduates, at the expense of research, travel, negotiating for grants, and so forth;

second, faculty members would become interested in attracting students to their classes; and third, they would be concerned that students completed their studies and obtained their degrees within a reasonable period of time. These three pressures would increase teaching productivity in universities, especially in undergraduate programs. Such productivity increases should outweigh the cost-increasing effects of workload reductions when professors' unions succeed in decreasing maximum class size and should temper any inclination on the part of university faculty to seek a reduction in maximum class hours per week.

Our conclusion, then, is that faculty organization and collective bargaining would increase the productivity of teaching university undergraduates. If the pressure to meet quantifiable standards of teaching proficiency is too great, however, the *quality* of teaching may suffer, as may the quality of degrees. Frequently teachers of great intellectual prowess and renown demand a great deal of students and consequently have small classes. For the few who are able to stand up to the pressure, attendance in such classes is a rare privilege. Yet such behavior on the part of a faculty member might not be condoned under collective bargaining agreements. Likewise, the pressure to ensure that as many students as possible obtain degrees without delay might lead to a lowering of academic degree requirements. Thus the short-run gains in faculty productivity might have to be discounted, but no one knows by how much. In addition, if the concentration of faculty energy on teaching makes universities less attractive places for highly talented persons to pursue their careers, the long-term effects might be to lower the quality of faculty and to increase the real costs of higher education (see Nerlove, 1972, pp. 204-211, for an interesting theoretical development of this point). Furthermore, research and graduate education are usually considered indivisible, but because research would no longer be of paramount importance, the productivity of faculty in graduate teaching might fall.

In considering other possible results of unionization, we must take into account a powerful external force for change, the oversupply of talented, well-qualified young men and women seeking appointments in universities. The market for Ph.D.s is bad, partly because undergraduate enrollment is leveling out and universities are not increasing faculty appointments. This situation will probably attract younger faculty members into the union movement. In exchange for their support of collective bargaining, younger faculty will expect benefits, though they will probably seek benefits related more to stability of employment than to salaries, sabbaticals, and so forth. First, they will seek earlier tenure, with the award possibly reflecting the completion of a certain number of years of satisfactory teaching experience. Second, they will favor open admissions to raise student enrollment and create more faculty positions. (It is not at all certain, however, that collective bargaining will free additional money for scholarships; hence some students who enter under an open admissions policy may find it difficult to perform well and support themselves financially at the same time. Unfortunately, then, an open admissions policy may in effect become a "revolving door" policy.) Third, younger faculty will support continuing education, community action, and extension programs to increase enrollments. Fourth, they will support liberal pension plans, in the hope of encouraging senior faculty to retire early. Pension liberalization, moreover, has two other points in its favor. It is a good issue on which to win the support of senior faculty, and, in the short run, large, dramatic increases in pensions, ordinarily subject to amortization, place a very small financial burden on the employer, although long-range costs are great. In 1972, for example, the New York State Commission on the Quality, Cost, and Financing of Elementary and Secondary Education drew public attention for the first time to the large future costs, running into billions of dollars, of the 1969 New York City agreement on pensions with the United Federation of Teachers (UFT). These costs have not yet been recognized in the city budget.

If one assumes that for the purposes of collective bargaining the primary measure of a faculty member's worth is his proficiency and industry in teaching and that all kinds of teaching are equally important, then it would be unjustified for certain departments to be allocated proportionally more resources than others based on their enrollments. For example, it would no longer be justified on grounds of the special costs of research to give the physics department a bigger budget per faculty member than the French department. Likewise, members of law and medical faculties would be under greater pressure to justify their off-scale pay rates (Wollett, 1971). Finally, if the chief function of the university was teaching—demonstrated by its being the basis for faculty promotion—how could the differences in pay and workload between universities, four-year colleges, and community colleges be defended? Collective bargaining might well bring about a great democratization in higher education, but as it did, individual research and Ph.D. programs would be deemphasized.

Whether the university would become more active in the political arena and whether it would devote a larger share of its resources to the analysis of questions of immediate social concern (pollution, racism, youth unemployment) and a smaller share to research of long-term consequences (pure research) seem to depend on the extent to which students become involved in the process of collective bargaining (for a pessimistic view of this possibility, see Ladd and Lipset, 1973, pp. 94-95). There are indications that students are becoming aware of the power the bargaining process could give them. Three collective bargaining agreements in Massachusetts during the fall of 1973 included students in the bargaining discussions as third parties, and a student strike over increased tuition at the University of Michigan almost occurred during the same time. In addition, state and national student lobby movements are increasing in influence and could become another pressure point for broad student involvement in collective bargaining. Students are legitimate parties of interest in negotiations, but the problem may be to adapt the traditional labor-vs.-management approach of trade unionism to the complex interplay of multiple forces and interests in higher education. Recent increases in statewide collective bargaining agreements with few local options may also indicate another source for student involvement in the bargaining process. If this should happen, then the consequences of negotiations would extend far beyond our simple prediction that conventional instructional services will be offered more democratically.

Increasing Efficiency

What measures might college and university administrators take to improve the technological efficiency of higher education if they had the full support of their faculties, organized or not? If administrators were free to make the decisions, what could they do to increase the technological efficiency of their operations?

Manipulation of Incentive Structure. Consider the example of a major university with English, French, history, and other liberal arts departments which are responsible for the instruction of both undergraduates and graduates. Undergraduates are required to take a certain number of courses offered in a general field such as foreign languages. The market for new Ph.D.s in this and comparable universities is limited.

If university administrators do not interfere with the faculty incentive structure, what can be expected? In major universities faculty are rewarded for significant research and writing in their fields. When they are successful, they are given promotions and honors within their own universities, they obtain fellowships and other awards from national academic bodies, and they are invited to read papers at international meetings. In contrast to such scholarly activity, which may be exciting and pleasurable and is at least directed toward the improvement of one's career, the administrative chores of serving on admissions committees or finding job openings for graduates are distasteful, especially when they demand much time.

In their research and writing, faculty enjoy the assistance of well-trained, eager graduate students who come fresh to the field and suggest new ideas. They have time to read and criticize the writings of colleagues and rivals; they are willing to perform the less interesting chores of looking up sources, editing manuscripts, and checking dates, tables, and quotations; and they are candidates for enrollment in the professor's graduate courses. The more senior the graduate student, the more able he or she is to take the most esoteric courses the professor can offer. By offering advanced courses, the faculty member is able to maintain his interest in teaching, a certain amount of which he or she is required to do in any case.

The member of the department also seeks a large number of graduate students to work as part-time teaching assistants in the basic courses that are required of undergraduates in the department. The yield for the department is twofold: full-time faculty are relieved of some of the tedious teaching chores, and graduate students are better off financially during their period of apprenticeship.

The graduate student, naturally enough, expects eventually to move beyond apprenticeship to journeyman status, the point of transition being the award of the doctorate. It is not necessarily in the faculty member's interest, however, for all his students to receive the Ph.D. degree—only the best ones. Because the market for Ph.D.s in any university is limited, a faculty member can expect to place only a small number of graduates, presumably the best, in institutions of comparable quality. If the professor encourages a large number of them to proceed rapidly toward their degrees, some will have to accept positions in inferior institutions and word will spread among students the professor cannot find any good jobs for students. This kind of rumor discourages the best junior graduate students from seeking the professor out as an adviser. A cycle of deterioration sets in—fewer good students, fewer interesting courses, less rigorous research published—that can harm the professor's career (Breneman, 1970a, 1970b, 1971).

Thus the incentive structure has two major characteristics: pressure on the department to enroll large numbers of graduate students, and reluctance on the part of individual faculty members to see any substantial number of their advisees complete the requirements for the Ph.D. Many students, then, after several years of service to the department, are finally turned away from the degree by such statements as "You really would not be well advised to take your orals" or "I am sorry to say that your recent advanced work raises serious doubt about your ability to write an acceptable dissertation—perhaps you should look for a job in a junior college." This incentive structure, with pressures to enroll large numbers of students but to see that few graduate, clearly produces technological inefficiency.

The output measure for instruction in graduate departments in major universities is the number of Ph.D.s awarded. A proper measure of technological efficiency in Ph.D. production would be the average number of student years for each degree awarded, assuming a constant average quality of graduates. Student time spent is valuable as a measure of all instructional resources consumed by a university during any period. The department described in this example would consume many years of student time for each degree it awarded because successful candidates would be kept in apprenticeship for so long and unsuccessful candidates would put in so many years before they were discouraged.

If administrators had a free hand, they would change the incentive structure. Specifically, the administration could create enrollment quotas for graduate students in each department, making the quotas a function of the speed and regularity with which each department produced degree holders (a similar quota system was introduced at the University of California in 1971). The mechanism might be to give points for degrees awarded (fewer for M.A.s than Ph.D.s) and demerits for each graduate student year after some minimum, perhaps two, not marked by some measure of progress such as the M.A., advancement to candidacy, passing the oral examination, or award of the Ph.D. A special demerit would be given when students who had spent years in the department left without completing their degrees. The student enrollment quota could then be used to determine how many new faculty places the department was entitled to, with undergraduate enrollments weighted less than graduate enrollments because undergraduate majors and courses are a matter of student choice.

Departments in major universities like to pursue new directions of inquiry and must be able occasionally to hire new faculty. But faculty places are tied to enrollments and enrollments are tied in part to productivity in awarding graduate degrees. In addition, graduate departments like to receive grants, for grants bring recognition, travel, and secretarial assistance. However, programs funded by granting agencies, foundations, and governments often demand additional staffing, which results in more pressure for expanding enrollments to earn these new faculty places.

Recalling that graduates are needed to serve as teaching and research assistants and that graduate enrollments are directly linked to the award of graduate degrees, we find a new emphasis placed on the completion of graduate work. The special penalty against the department for a student's failure after long residence assures that departments will not attempt to maintain enrollments by prolonging the work of potentially unsuccessful students. But any hasty weeding out of unproven students must also be avoided.

The fear that this shift in the incentive structure will lower the quality of graduate degrees is unfounded because many of the old incentives remain even after the shift. Faculty do not want to see their students win their degrees with unprofessional dissertations because well-reputed institutions will not hire them, and the personal and professional deterioration we mentioned above will set in. Rather, three results are likely. First, faculty will select students who are likely to complete their degrees; second, they will become more active in finding good jobs for their students; third, in departments with slim markets for their Ph.D.s, faculty will assume greater responsibility for teaching lower division courses and carrying out the details of their research work. In sum, a shift in the incentive structure would persuade faculty to work hard in both their administrative and their professional capacities.

Introduction of Educational Technology. The operating expenditures of colleges and universities using traditional methods of instruction have shown a strong rising trend. Between 1958-1959 and 1967-1968, the overall price index for instructional operating expenditures rose from 100 to 148.5. The greatest rise in a major cost component was in faculty salaries, where the price index rose from 100 in 1958-1959 to 173.5 in 1967-1968 (O'Neill, 1971). Aside from the additional expenditures caused by inflation, colleges and universities constantly need to purchase additional equipment for science laboratories and books and periodicals for their libraries. The advance of knowledge itself dictates these expenditures. Rises in prices, especially the price of faculty services, combined with the need for ever-increasing amounts of instructional goods, easily explain increases in costs per credit hour of instruction. In current dollars, costs per credit hour in all institutions went up from $38.45 in 1958-1959 to $50.10 in 1966-1967 (O'Neill, 1971). The costs of traditional instruction are projected to rise further in the future.

However, it now appears likely that traditional instructional processes can be modified to control costs by introducing physical capital in place of faculty time. Current indications point toward a reduction in the cost per credit hour if computer-assisted instruction (CAI) is used, as measured against continued increases in the price of faculty time. By substituting a means of instruction with a downward price trend for one with a persistent upward trend, universities can keep costs down.

We are not proposing that physical capital be substituted for human capital in the production of educational services if the end result is a decline in program quality measured, say, by how much students learn. Plainly, certain departments are especially vulnerable to a loss of quality when physical capital is introduced. Mechanization of instruction in the visual arts, except perhaps in art appreciation courses, is probably not feasible and certainly not desirable. Experiments in different universities —Florida State University, the State University of New York at Stony Brook, the University of Illinois, the University of Texas, and Stanford University—indicate however that in fields such as mathematics, physics, chemistry, and foreign languages, one hour of CAI can be substituted for one hour of conventional classroom instruction with no measurable loss of learning on the part of students.

The costs of CAI have been declining for two reasons. First, CAI is subject to technological advances since the computer industry is strongly committed to research and development and computer capacity, for example, tends to increase with the square of product price. Second, when CAI is made available to large numbers of students, fixed costs are lower per student. In 1965 total CAI costs per student contact hour, including depreciation, maintenance of computers and terminals, communication between central computers and terminals, staff for designing and testing instructional programs, and university overhead, were about three dollars; in 1972 they had decreased to about one dollar. Future advances in CAI technology, plus wide use of CAI by students, should allow further cost reduction.

Taking into account the relationship between contact hours and credit hours, the proportion of faculty time now spent in traditional classroom instruction, and the overall costs of classroom instruction, the cost of CAI per credit hour and the cost of faculty time per credit hour in the classroom are approximately equal. Further reduction in CAI costs would provide colleges and universities with at least two options: to reduce the instructional budget per student by substituting machines for faculty, or to shift faculty time from classroom work to individualized types of instruction in which the scarce skills of faculty presumably would be used intensively, at a smaller incremental cost than could be achieved without the use of CAI.

Summary

During the 1960s, it was hoped that colleges and universities could become technologically more efficient through the scientific analysis of their production processes. Planning-programing-budgeting systems represent an attempt to bring the discipline and the evaluation methods of business into the public sector and into public or private higher education. But the experience with PPBS has been disappointing. There is still little agreement about what the priorities for the allocation of college and university resources should be. Knowledge about the production processes of higher education remains vague in the extreme, a result, in part, of the intractable difficulties of measuring inputs and outputs.

However, we see an increasing inclination for college and university administrators and faculty to use policy analysis in their own institutions. Program accounting, or the identification of resource commitment to specific functions—the teaching of lower division mathematics for example—is growing apace. It allows constructive comparisons to be made between changing resource commitments in different institutions. Colleges and universities increasingly use simulation models to estimate the financial consequences of different events and policies. The faculty incentive structure in different departments is also being analyzed to test whether it serves its purpose. Thus, though PPBS has not given us an overall framework for regulating the allocation of college and university resources, policy analysis is flourishing as never before. Colleges and universities are more and more subject to faculty collective bargaining. Because it is itself a means of determining resource allocation, collective bargaining is a force that will affect the technological efficiency of higher education. Policy analysis is one way that college and university administrators have to strengthen their hand at the bargaining table, when they confront the demands of organized faculty.

We predict that collective bargaining in the university will have a major effect in establishing new power alignments. Faculty in the inner circle of power in major universities have in the past attained their eminence primarily from their research. It is likely that this group will have to give way to a coalition of older faculty interested in teaching and younger faculty in general. The university reward structure is likely in the future to be based on proficiency—or at least zeal—in classroom duties. In the short run, then, collective bargaining may well have the effect of raising the level of technological efficiency in undergraduate instruction. Whether it will have more profound effects on universities will depend on whether students become deeply involved in negotiations.

3

Paying for the Learning Society

Fiscal efficiency in higher education is achieved by minimizing reliance on taxes while fulfilling social objectives. A serious debate has emerged about the amount and form of public subsidy for higher education (Hartman, 1971). One position is that higher education should be free to the student in the same way that elementary and secondary education is free. Others argue that students should bear the full cost of the services of higher education so that the objective of fiscal efficiency may be achieved.

Although these two arguments are at opposite poles, they are by no means extreme. Free education in the United States means that the instructional costs of higher education are fully subsidized by public monies. In effect, free higher education implies zero tuition. But the expense to the student of obtaining higher education includes his foregone income, a sum usually in excess of direct instructional costs (Hansen and Weisbrod, 1969). In response to this loss of income, British and European governments subsidize not only the cost of instruction but also living expenses. A more complete approach would be to compensate the student completely for the money he could make, by full- or part-time employment, if he were not attending a college or university. This procedure would allow a person to be a student and at the same time support dependent children, siblings, or parents. We discuss this kind of governmental policy in the next chapter.

The opposite position, that a student pay the full cost of the services he receives, is also not as extreme as one might think. If colleges and universities became proprietary institutions, they might become more efficient and flexible and possibly would attract more highly talented persons as faculty. Regardless of the justification, fees charged to students would cover not only the costs of instruction but also profit to the owners of these institutions.

Charging fees in excess of actual instructional costs can also be defended on egalitarian grounds. Assume that the benefits of higher education go to the individual and that college-educated persons typically receive incomes that are higher than can be justified by the costs they have incurred in going to college. What could be fairer than to charge the college student an extra fee for the privilege of going to college and to distribute the money to those who are not qualified to attend? Yet policies of charging fees in excess of the costs of higher education lack political appeal.

Full-Cost Pricing

This chapter explores the rationale behind full-cost pricing, a policy under which colleges and universities fully cover their instructional costs by charging students fees. Proposals for full-cost pricing are commonly accompanied by proposals for expanding student loan plans, which may also be considered as devices for shifting the costs of higher education to the student (but not his parents). Loan or credit mechanisms allow the student to spread the "lumpy" expenditures (concentrated during just a few years) for advanced schooling over a more extended period.

The subsidy of higher education, such as occurs when state governments meet a large share of the costs of running public colleges and universities, can lead to misallocations of economic resources. If we assume for the sake of initial argument that colleges and universities provide benefits only to individuals, and that all families in the country have equal incomes, then the case for full-cost pricing can be put as follows (Danière, 1964, pp. 13-14):

Take a country made up of five million families, each with a child of college age. At full-cost tuition ($2000), we find that four million attend college. If the tuition is reduced to $1500, however, all five million are ready to enroll. In which case is the country better off? Barring philanthropy, educational institutions can function under reduced tuition only if the state subsidizes them up to $500 per student. This amount ($2.5 billion) must come out of taxes which, if the burden is distributed equally among all families, will cost each of them $500. For the economy as a whole, the shift from full-cost to reduced tuition has resulted in putting two billion dollars more (one million students costing $2000 each) of the nation's resources into education and two billion dollars less in other goods and services. This cut is effected by having one million newly enrolled students put $1500 in education and $500 in taxes which they previously spent otherwise. The students previously enrolled lost $500 in taxes but pay $500 less in tuition and can afford exactly the same purchases as before.

The welfare implications of the shift are now clear. The four million original students are as well off as before while the additional one million have lost. The latter are indeed enjoying a college education rather than the $2000 of other goods and services they previously consumed, but we know from their previous refusal to enroll at full tuition that an education to them is worth less than the alternative $2000 basket. This fact is not erased by their decision—after being independently taxed $500—to take an education rather than $1500 only of other goods and services. We must therefore conclude that overall welfare has been reduced by the imposition of tuitions below costs.

Under a suitable system of taxes and transfers —and if we persist in treating higher education as a regular consumer good (meaning, *inter alia,* that education generates no social benefits)—it will be found that some overall improvement of welfare is in general possible by shifting from a tuition below or above cost to one representing the full cost.

If we now acknowledge that higher education does generate social benefits and that households really have different incomes, it might appear to destroy the case for full-cost pricing. If we recognize that all higher education benefits society, then we must be concerned that our neighbor's child, as well as our own, receives enough education. But full-cost tuition may discourage our neighbors from participating, whether by choice or lack of sufficient income. Further, according to the criterion of fairness, we may wish to see low-income youth attend colleges and universities. Yet recognizing the social benefits of higher education does not destroy the theoretical case for full-cost pricing; it simply modifies it.

West (1970) has dealt thoroughly with the relation between public goods and services, or those yielding social benefits, and pricing. He argues that in providing social benefits, minimum standards of service are the key variables to manipulate. For example, it may matter very little for generating social benefits whether a potential scientist attends Berkeley or Yale, but the costs of maintaining the future scientist in the first institution are about half of those in the second. The potential scientist should attend an institution where he or she can develop professional abilities; beyond this, the general public need not be concerned to see the young man or woman participate in the cultural life of his or her society.

The second part of the argument is that the minimum standards for generating social benefits should be obtained under minimum taxation because taxation, as a form of compulsion, represents an interference with the process by which a family distributes its income among goods and services in the private marketplace to maximize its satisfactions. Therefore, whatever amount of higher education that provides for social benefits should be obtained at minimum public expense. If we assume that rich families will purchase for their children more than enough educational services to satisfy the minimum required to generate social benefits, then any system of institutional grants or vouchers to all students regardless of income is likely to encourage these families to contribute less to the support of higher education than they would otherwise. Accordingly, a system of financing higher education that fails to recognize differences in household income and in the capacity to pay for the cost of instruction from private sources is bound to require more taxes than are necessary.

The form of the financial mechanism is important. As West has stated, "lump-grant/vouchers and price subsidies normally have separately distinguishable effects. . . . (The latter) enlists the substitution effect in (a person's) preference system as well as the income effect in favor of an increase in his consumption" (534-536). The difference can be illustrated by an arithmetic example. Suppose a family has one child ready to enter college and faces a choice between a private university costing $4000 a year and a free public university that is spending $2000 a year per student. Free tuition at the public university is a lump grant, since the amount is independent of the family's own contribution. It can also be considered as an education voucher worth $2000, issued to all families in the state with college-age children. Assuming the family prefers the private university, if it estimates $3000 as the maximum it can pay for tuition, then under the conditions stated, it must, in the absence of private scholarship aid, enroll the child in the public university.

Now, suppose the state adopts a policy under which it meets twenty-five percent of all households' educational expenditures. In this case, the family would choose the private university, accepting a price subsidy of $1000 from the state and paying $3000 from its own resources. This shift in the finance mechanism would have the following result: expenditure on higher education would rise by $2000 and public support funds from taxes would fall by $1000.

One way to minimize taxation to obtain the social benefits of education is what West (pp. 539-540) calls the "constitutional approach":

> Each individual is treated as a choice-maker in the selection from basic sets of legal frameworks. . . . Imagine a new community settlement of young immigrant adults wherein no children had yet been born and no constitution had yet been laid down. Each adult would now have to consider

not only his future private utility of having children but also the potential disutility from the "undesirable" behavior or appearance of the neighbor's children. Since the neighbor will be in the reverse position (fearing the potential disutility from one's own children) a constitutional rule may be agreed to, laying down the conditions in which privileges of parenthood may be conferred. One of these conditions will be that each parent will supply up to a given minimum of education, food, clothing and so on, from his own income resources. If society depended *exclusively* on these conditions to protect children and to provide sufficient external (social) benefits, then no subsidies, income transfers, or price reductions would be necessary for any of the goods and services mentioned. Because of the anticipated legal responsibilities adults would be discouraged from marriage or parenthood until such a time as they can afford to bring their children up in conformity with the minimum constitutional standards previously laid down.

Plainly, such an "ideal situation" is not likely to develop. A workable alternative, granting the objective of minimizing taxation for higher education, is to adopt a system of price subsidies under which families above a certain income level would pay full costs and all other families would pay a progressively smaller proportion, depending on their incomes.

Empirical support for the need for this alternative is presented by Hansen and Weisbrod (1969) in the major study to date of who pays for and who benefits from public higher education. Table 1 is a summary of that study.

Although there are different interpretations of the Hansen-Weisbrod data, it is generally agreed, as we shall see in the next chapter, that California's subsidies of public higher education are regressive. The richer the family, the greater the possibility that it will receive a large subsidy; the poorer the family, the greater the probability that it will receive a small amount of subsidy. The basic reasons for this situation are easy to see: college attendance is positively related to social class; eligibility to attend the more expensive institutions, which are subject to

Table 1

REGRESSIVENESS OF HIGHER EDUCATION SUBSIDIES
IN CALIFORNIA

	All Families	Families with No Children in System	Families with Children in		
			Junior College	State College	University
Income	8,000	7,900	8,800	10,000	12,000
Subsidy	—	0	720	1,400	1,700
Taxes	620	650	680	770	910
Net gain (loss)	—	(650)	40	630	790

Source: Hansen and Weisbrod, 1969, p. 76.

large public subsidy, such as the nine campuses of the University of California, is also positively related to social class; and finally, social class is positively related to income.

If one regards regressivity in the distribution of higher education subsidies as a social evil, then the radical approach to the problem is to change the basic conditions noted above that give rise to it. A more conventional, and probably more workable, approach is to suggest reform in the system of finance. The objective of reform is a realignment of net gain or loss, so that they become inversely related to household income. Thus Hansen and Weisbrod (1969, p. 101) propose that a possible source of funds for the needy would be those college students and families "who are able and willing to pay more than the efficient price of education. If they were charged a higher price, the subsidies required could be obtained outside the tax system. That is, higher income families would pay more tuition, with the extra funds being made available to permit lower payments for low income students. This would amount to the use of classic price discrimination, to charge what the traffic will bear. One might think of the resulting schedule of charges as reflecting a sliding scale college payment plan, with the possibility of negative charges for the most needy."

This kind of financial reform would almost certainly produce net gain or loss inverse to household income among families with children in college. To that extent, it would induce a larger number of the qualified poor to enter colleges and universities. This reform, however, does little in any direct way to reduce the correlation between social class and income or that between social class and the eligibility to enter academically superior institutions.

In any case, it seems unlikely that a sliding scale of fees, under which richer families pay more than the full cost of higher education, would be workable. There is no special reason why parents with children attending public institutions should, if they are rich enough, be asked to support the further schooling of the disadvantaged. Perhaps this social cost should be spread over all richer families generally, but then we would need to rely on progressive income taxes to achieve that result. One of the objectives of our present argument, however, is to avoid heavy reliance on such compulsory levies. Also, because children now become legal adults at age eighteen, it seems unrealistic, considering the new legal status of college students and their apparent desire to become independent of their parents at a younger age than before, to expect to solve the problem of financing higher education by laying the entire burden on parents.

There is reason to think, moreover, that a graduated scale of fees (according to parental income) in state institutions would push richer youth into private colleges and universities. "For the educational system as a whole, there would be a decrease in the average wealth of students' families and most likely an increase in the average quality of students. The state university, however, would become more of a 'poor man's' school and the private university more of a 'rich man's' school. Many would consider this increased homogeneity to be contrary to the objective of a democratic society and detrimental to the educational process" (Burns and Chiswick, 1970, p. 245).

The most recent report on financing of higher education in New York State (New York State, Task Force on Financing Higher Education, 1973) proposes a system of grants scaled by parental income that would establish, in effect, a graduated price structure for higher education. Grants would be available for attendance at private institutions as well as public. Those for attendance at private institutions would be much higher than for public. For example, a typical family with income of $14,000 would receive a grant from the state of $1180 for each of its children attending a private residential college, but nothing at all for each of its children attending a public institution. At the same time, the task force recommended that the City University of New York, long a bastion of zero-cost tuition, levy fees of at least $650 per year. However, since low-income students more easily gain admission to public institutions than private, and since these New York proposals reduce the financial disincentive for middle-class families to send their children to private institutions, this particular price scaling mechanism would probably make private institutions more clearly "rich men's schools" while at the same time directing state subsidy toward the middle class at the expense of the poor.

In principle, one way to establish a progressive system of higher education finance without taxation is to charge students the full cost of their instruction, while arranging at the same time a loan plan under which economically successful graduates would return more to the loan bank than they have borrowed. The other side of the coin, of course, is that low-income graduates would be allowed to escape payment altogether for some part of the costs of their higher education. These so-called "income-contingent" student loans could increase the fiscal efficiency of higher education by allowing a shift of the $15 billion cost now borne by taxpayers to the students themselves. Moreover, such loans would be at least superficially progressive. Under the loan plan, graduates who obtain the most financial gain from attending college would be required to transfer part of their incremental earnings to graduates who were not particularly successful or who chose to enter low-paying, but possibly socially useful, occupations. In the remainder of this chapter, we shall consider some income-contingent loan proposals, plans now in operation, and the strengths and weaknesses of such programs as instruments of social policy.

Income-Contingent Student Loans

The Educational Finance Corporation. In his sophisticated income-contingent loan proposal, Vickrey (1962, p. 268)
notes that the U.S. has failed to find a proper plan for financing
education to the full extent of people's own capabilities. He
believes that expansion of public higher education is not the
complete answer, because even when public institutions charge
low fees, low-income students do not have enough money to
support themselves or buy books and other school supplies.
Furthermore, while the vitality of American higher education
depends in part on the continued existence of private institutions, public investment in public institutions does nothing directly to strengthen the private sector. Nor does it provide poor
youth access to private institutions, even though they might
greatly profit from instruction in private institutions.

Vickrey observes that the classic answer to such a problem is offering loans to those who show such promise that
investment in their education would yield at least the normal
rate of return on a comparably risky investment. "While this
proposal is . . . developed in some detail," he states, "it is not
suggested as an exclusive solution to the problem of financing
higher education. Rather, it is a scheme which, if implemented,
would supplement other institutional arrangements for such
financing. While the more familiar sources of support for institutions of higher education need to be expanded, and aid to
students greatly enlarged, there is also need for new financial
arrangements to facilitate the flow of capital into development
of human resources."

Conventional student loan schemes have serious draw-
backs. First, since a loan must be repaid in full with a stated
rate of interest, independent of a person's rate of earnings, students are reluctant to saddle themselves with large fixed debts.
The repayment obligation, in annual cash flow, can be reduced
by extending the period of amortization; this is important because earnings in early years of employment tend to be low
compared to the size of household obligations. Lenders are reluctant, however, to make extremely long-term loans because of

the high cost of enforcing claims for repayment over many years, costs that are amplified by the geographic mobility of the population. Second, loans are frequently advanced in a spirit of philanthropy and carry the stigma of charity. Third, loans are often severely rationed. "Where the burden of repayment can become substantial," Vickrey writes, "it is natural to protect the applicant from getting in too deep; where there is an element of subsidy in the loan, the worthiness of the applicant becomes a consideration." More than ten years later, his observation is still germane. Porter (1973) notes that "rarely has the squeeze on the student from the middle-income family been more severe." Two important reasons are high interest rates, which cause banks to divert funds to more profitable uses, and action by the government to restrict the family income limit under which a student may qualify for subsidized loans; in most cases the family income ceiling for eligibility has moved downward from $15,000 to $10,000. Finally, in cases where both spouses work and one would prefer to stay at home and do housework, the loan represents a "negative dowry," that is, an obligation accepted by the husband or wife to pay back the costs of his or her spouse's college education.

As an alternative to conventional loan plans, how would Vickrey's plan work? The borrower would agree to return dividends on any extra income he earned because of the additional amount of higher education he had completed. If a young person had completed the program of a community college and wished to transfer to a four-year institution in order to study for the B.A. degree, he would arrange financing for the third and fourth years of his college program, the "additional amount" of higher education. One estimate would be made of his expected lifetime earnings based on the completion of community college, and a second estimate based on the completion of the B.A. The difference between these two estimates—presumably a positive figure—would be the "extra income" attributable to this additional amount of higher education. Estimates would be prepared by college and university administrators under guidelines developed by an "Educational Finance Corporation" that would be responsible for the general administration of the program. Obviously, administrators would need a considerable amount of data about earnings potentials in various occupations, the relationship between such earnings and graduates' grade point averages, the predictive ability of test scores and other measurement tools, and so on.

One projection would be made of the candidate's estimated earnings with his existing education. A second projection would be made of his potential earnings with the additional education for which he seeks to borrow money. For each $1000 borrowed, the student would pledge to pay a certain rate of tax on all income in excess of his estimated earnings with existing education. The tax schedule, according to Vickrey, should be progressive.

For example, suppose our hypothetical community college graduate is estimated to earn $12,000 per year in the first five years of his working life. The borrower might under his loan contract be required to pay the Educational Finance Corporation a sum equal to 0.5 percent of his earnings between $12,000 and $13,999, 1.0 percent of earnings between $14,000 and $15,999, 1.5 percent of earnings in excess of $16,000, and so on. The complete plan would deal not just with the first five years but with his entire working life. Both the existing and potential earnings projections would rise over time to some maximum, but the schedule of dividend rates set when the individual received his final payment would remain constant for his whole working life. Vickrey recommends that the repayment rates be set at such a level that if the borrower's income during his or her working life equals his potential earnings projection—in other words, if the prediction works out precisely—he or she would repay the corporation the amount borrowed, plus 9 percent interest. A contract would be set up for each student separately, with repayment rates varying from one student to the next, depending on how much potential earnings projections exceeded existing earnings projections. Some students would return to the corporation a greater yield on the corporation's investment than nine percent, and others, those who never earned more than their existing earnings projection, might return nothing at all. (The assets of the Educational Finance Corporation would be protected by mutualization of risks, the process of offsetting losses from persons who earn less than expected with returns from those who earn more.) Lifetime earnings in excess of potential earnings projections would represent a subsidy payment from the individual to the corporation; likewise, earnings below potential earnings projections would produce a subsidy to the individual from the corporation. If all worked out as intended, the total of subsidies provided *to* the Corporation by the more financially successful graduates would equal approximately the total of subsidies provided *by* the corporation to the less successful.

The Vickrey plan is a dynamic one. Each year of a student's education would produce new information about his projected earnings. Each year a new contract would be offered to the student with revised dividend rates. (The revised rates would apply, of course, only if the student borrowed additional funds; a student whose prospects had diminished would not find himself saddled with higher dividend rates on his old debt.) Most likely, however, the recomputation would show improved return, and the student would be offered funds to continue his education; if he did not benefit from continued education, he would not have to pay for it.

Certain additional features of the plan should be noted. The contract would specify that borrowers, if requested, would supply the corporation with copies of their federal income tax returns on a confidential basis, to ensure the safety of the operation of the plan. Also, those borrowers with good earning records would accumulate retirement benefits. After the corporation had been repaid with a stated rate of interest, all future dividends would flow into a retirement fund for those borrowers. Particularly successful persons might be granted retirement allowances at higher than average rates.

What are the virtues and defects of this particular version of income-contingent student loans? We will concentrate first on its virtues. First, the plan offers generous loans, equal to fees plus foregone income. If students were not bothered by the requirements to pay earning dividends to the corporation over their working life—a large assumption, by the way—then the plan would remove existing financial barriers to college attendance by potential college enrollees. Second, the progressiveness of dividend rates and the requirement that individuals pay earnings dividends over their total working lives appear to make the plan progressive in incidence. Third, the fact that dividend rates are a function of an individual's apparent success as a student (which is, in turn, taken to be a prediction of financial success in the marketplace) establishes a strong incentive for academic diligence. Fourth, the plan avoids the problem of negative dowry, since individuals who do not work are not required to repay at all.

The primary defect of the plan is characteristic of all voluntary income-contingent plans, regressivity. Even though Vickrey's plan has a mildly progressive schedule of dividend rates, and even though a financially successful individual is required to contribute to the corporation over his whole working life, we may be certain that the process of individual rating will establish an underlying regressivity in financing. Students who are doing satisfactory but not outstanding work in college, law school, business school, and so forth, would receive lower projections of their potential earnings than students near the top of their classes. Students whose work was only marginally acceptable would be assigned even lower projections of potential earnings. Because the financial value of academic excellence increases exponentially with the length of education, projections of the potential earnings of students with different educational records would be much more variable than projections of their estimated earnings with existing education. Since dividend rates decrease as the gap between potential and existing earnings projections becomes wider, students with poorer records will be assigned higher repayment rates than good students.

As we have already noted, college eligibility and performance are both functionally related to social class. This means that since students from low-income households average fewer college years and lower performance, they would end up paying higher average dividend rates than students from middle- and high-income families. Students with the advantage of lower dividend rates also have the advantage of their backgrounds—they qualify far more easily than poorer students. Thinking of dividend rates as a user charge for higher education that is at the same time a peculiar type of income tax—peculiar because each individual has his own rate schedule—we see that Vickrey has proposed an income tax under which poor families typically would be assigned higher rate schedules than rich families. The fact that the structure of rates is progressive, in that the higher one's income is, the higher the tax rate on it is, should not disguise the fact that persons with poorer than average income prospects are required to pay tax under a higher than average rate schedule.

Exactly the same argument can be made with respect to persons who choose low-income occupations. Many low-income callings, such as those of teacher or nurse in rural areas, are the ones that urgently need recruits. People from low-income families who choose to work in poverty neighborhoods at socially demanding but low-paying jobs would seem to be especially disadvantaged under the Vickrey plan.

Another problem concerns how values for existing and potential earnings projections are to be established; this is a crucial point, since repayment rates are computed on the basis of these values. According to Vickrey, ratings would be based on grades, test scores, and other evidence of educational potential. It is unclear whether test scores and grades are truly correlated to predictions of future earning potential.

Lastly, the size of payment made by a person to the corporation is a function not only of his particular rate schedule but also of the total amount of his borrowing. (The repayment or dividend rates apply to each $1000 borrowed.) Poor students would probably need to borrow more than rich because they would receive less money from their parents and relatives, and because they would have greater difficulty in obtaining summer employment. Poor students who wished to attend prestigious private universities might have to borrow especially large amounts. Vickrey himself has indicated that repayment rates can reach staggering heights. "In an extreme case a student who went through seven years of undergraduate and graduate training and contracted for the maximum advance obtainable would

be receiving advances ranging from $4000 for freshman year
... to $8000 for the third year of graduate work, a total of
$38,500; in return for this he would be contracting for earnings-
dividend payments on a scale ranging up to 57 3/4 percent on
that part of his income in excess of $10,000 for the years in.
which his earnings are expected to reach their average annual
lifetime level." Because of the repayment burden, it is almost
impossible to imagine that Vickrey's plan would completely
remove the influence of parental circumstances on college and
university enrollment.

    Regressivity is not an accidental feature of the Vickrey
plan. If income-contingent loan plans are to remain solvent,
they must attract clients who will go out in the world and make
a great deal of money. Otherwise the lending agency would
receive no surplus to offset the losses from loans to students
who turn out to be poor earners. Many persons are able to make
fairly accurate predictions of what their future earnings will be.
Someone who believes he will become rich is not likely to sign
up voluntarily in a loan plan that is going to tax him at a high
rate over a long period of time. If he must borrow, he always
has the option of a straight fixed-term loan. Thus the cost anticipated by an individual who enters an income-contingent
scheme can never exceed by very much the costs of his taking a
straight loan. Payments on income-contingent loans are, however, easier to meet in early earning years than those on straight
loans. All voluntary plans must therefore deal gently with the
future rich if they are to benefit from future earnings. For this
reason, they are all basically regressive.

    The Educational Opportunity Bank. The second plan we
consider is called the "Educational Opportunity Bank," known
also as the Zacharias plan (Panel on Educational Innovation,
1967). Its recommendations are, first, that this Educational Opportunity Bank be created as an agency of the federal government, with power to borrow money at going government rates
and to lend the proceeds of its own borrowings to students;
second, that any student be entitled to borrow enough money
to cover his fees, incidental costs, and subsistence at whatever
college, university, or other postsecondary institution he at-

tends; third, that in conjunction with federal income tax the borrower pay a specified percentage of his income to the bank, on the order of one percent of adjusted gross income for each $3000 borrowed, over a period of thirty years after graduation; and fourth, that borrowers be able, if they wished, to treat their loans as six percent obligations (that is, at any time they could opt out of the program by paying back the sums borrowed plus interest at six percent compounded annually.

Important differences exist between the Zacharias plan and the earlier Vickrey proposal. First, Zacharias argues for the establishment of an Educational Opportunity Bank as a federal agency, while Vickrey suggests that a private corporation be established to administer the student loan program. Since both agencies would be national in scope, this difference is not terribly significant. Two factors probably make the governmental approach preferable however. First, repayment could be coordinated with the filing of federal tax returns, reducing the cost of collection. Also, the Congress could more readily subsidize the operation of the loan plan as a federal agency, since as an arm of government such an agency could easily arrange for year-to-year changes in the rate of subsidy to protect students from the occasional sharp rises in interest rates that occur when government uses monetary policy (manipulation of bank reserves and interest rates) to combat inflation. The second difference is that the Zacharias plan defines the maximum level of borrowing as costs plus subsistence, while Vickrey defines it as costs plus foregone income. This difference is probably not significant in most cases; however, the Vickrey approach presumably would allow students pursuing advanced degrees to live a little more comfortably. Third, Zacharias would levy earnings dividends on total adjusted gross income, while Vickrey would grant a sizable exemption equal to foregone income at the time of last borrowing. On the surface this appears to allow the Educational Opportunity Bank to offer much lower dividend rates than Vickrey's, but the two sets of rates should be roughly equal when computed on the same income base. Vickrey's approach to the definition of income subject to repayment dividends takes care of the negative dowry problem, while Zacharias's plan leaves it unsolved. Fourth, Zacharias has a single dividend rate—approximately one percent of adjusted gross income for each $3000 borrowed, while Vickrey proposes a progressive rate. The latter would appear to be preferred, given the underlying regressivity of any income-contingent loan plan. Fifth, Zacharias allows higher earners to opt out by paying off their loans at six percent, while Vickrey would use individual ratings of future earnings to make each class of worker—high earner, middle earner, low earner—self-supporting in terms of its loan obligation. Both devices offer advantages to the rich and both are included for the same purpose—to make income-contingent loans sufficiently attractive to students with superior financial prospects that they join up and allow their good fortune to be shared by the less economically productive.

The important opt-out provision of the Zacharias plan received much attention from the panel (p. 11):

> In order to insure students against the risk of a low adult income, the bank must either make a profit on those students who earn high adult incomes or else obtain a Government subsidy. If the bank is to be self-sustaining, gains from high earners must offset losses on low earners. This raises the possibility that prospective high earners would most likely choose to finance their education in other ways, depressing the median income of the bank's borrowers and reducing the amount it could lend on a given percentage of future income. One solution would be to lend only to good risks. This would defeat a principal objective of the Bank. The other would be to make bank loans attractive even to those who have a good chance of doing very well. In order to do this the bank would have to come fairly close to matching the terms on which loans are at present available to such students. (It need not quite match them, since no student is certain he will become rich, and many with excellent prospects would be willing to pay something for the insurance feature, and the maximum amount available under present plans falls considerably short of maximum needs.) . . . Present federally guaranteed loans are repayable at six percent

annually, over ten years. . . . We therefore propose
that the bank allow its borrowers to treat their
debts as six percent loans if they wish.

The opt-out proposal does not quite match the six percent term loans because of some interest forgiveness features in
the existing federally insured program. This forgiveness applies
only to students from low-income families, however, hardly the
target group for the opt-out feature.

Which proposal, that of Zacharias or Vickrey, deals better
with the problem of avoiding excessive "adverse risk selection,"
that is, loading up membership in the loan plan with a disproportionate number of persons with low potential income? There
is no clear answer for such policy questions but certain considerations are worth noting. First, Vickrey claims that individual
assessment for dividend rate provides an extra incentive for students to take their studies seriously. The Zacharias proposal is
weaker on this point, for the advantage it provides for diligence
is opting out earlier, an uncertain prospect that is not nearly as
immediate as receiving a reduction in dividend rate while one is
still in college. Second, Zacharias's plan obviously has the virtue
of simplicity in administration; indeed, the feasibility, as well as
the propriety, of individual assessment in the Vickrey proposal
is questionable. Third, the Vickrey plan sets up differentially
high barriers against borrowing large sums for all but the talented
poor and for those who wish to enter low paying fields of
work. Zacharias's plan is free of this iniquity; thus, it is more
likely to help poor and socially minded youth attend expensive
private institutions if that is what they want to do.

If the Zacharias plan discriminates less harshly against the
present and future poor than the Vickrey proposal, it nevertheless remains regressive because of the opt-out feature. Consider
two students who each borrow $9000. The first student has a
steady adjusted gross income of $6000 for thirty years. Over
that thirty-year period, he annually contributes $180 to the
bank (one percent of income for each $3000 borrowed). Ab-
stracting from present value discounting, we see that our first
borrower pays off his loan at three percent of his income (he

would never repay his loan in full—only $5400 of it). The other student goes on to earn a steady $40,000 yearly adjusted gross income. After five years of making repayments of $1200, for a total of $6000, he chooses to opt out by paying off the remaining $3000 of his loan, plus six percent interest compounded annually, or $2200. In total, he would have paid $11,200 for his $9000 loan. This sum is only 0.9 percent of his thirty-year income. The richer person, then, pays "interest" at less than a one percent rate, while the poorer person must pay at three percent. Regressivity could be reduced by granting larger exemptions for Educational Opportunity Bank repayments than the Internal Revenue allows for personal income tax. This procedure would represent a combination of the Vickrey and Zacharias approaches—but without the feature of individual assessment (Shell, 1970).

Before concluding our discussion of the Zacharias plan, let us note some of the arguments advanced in its favor by the panel. In the first place, the Panel contrasted its own plan for income-contingent loans with previous government efforts to help finance higher education by pointing out the freedom of its proposed plan from any requirements to discriminate among recipients—always a difficult, politically sensitive process. "Our proposed program requires no one to decide between the rich and the poor, or among the merits of various cities, states, institutions, and so forth. It needs no peer-group evaluations, no political pressure, no compromises among the various aspects of civil rights" (p. vii).

Also, the Educational Opportunity Bank would make available larger amounts of money per student, because of the long period for repayment, and hence borrowers would not be as likely to get in over their heads. At the same time, the Bank would not hinder the expansion of other means of financing higher education, as for example a massive expansion of institutional grants would. Rather, it leaves other financial options completely open. The bank, moreover, offers another kind of fiscal neutrality: its existence in no way interferes with colleges' setting their expenditure priorities and developing their particular specialties.

The bank would allow students to exercise more choice in attending institutions. With access to bank loans, poor students might choose to go to residential colleges rather than local commuter colleges. The bank would place a larger share of responsibility for financing education in students' hands. Some students undoubtedly would welcome this opportunity to be financially independent of their parents. Parents, especially middle-class parents, would no longer need to pressure the government to count college costs as income tax deductions or credits. We regard this as a gain, for among the various methods for financing higher education, tax deductions and credits are especially regressive.

National Student Loan Bank. The Rivlin Report (U.S. Department of Health, Education and Welfare, 1969) has also proposed a scheme for income-contingent loans. Discussing their proposal for a "National Student Loan Bank," the authors of the report first draw attention to a major problem in the design of the Zacharias Educational Opportunity Bank.

> Because individuals probably do have reasonably good expectations about their expected income yields, a skewed distribution of entrants into the Educational Opportunity Bank loan fund can be almost guaranteed. The potential borrowers are more likely to be students from lower ability levels and from lower income groups if these attributes are correlated with lower income expectations. They are also more likely to be individuals who expect or plan to enter professions that are characteristically lower paying than the average professions entered by college graduates or attendees. Because of this skewed distribution of entrants, any attempt to make the Educational Opportunity Bank an unsubsidized loan program would demand that very high incremental repayment tax rates be charged to the loan program's participants. These high tax rates would, in addition to possibly distorting individuals' work-leisure decisions, tend to discourage potential borrowers from entering the Educational Opportunity Bank program unless no other alternatives were in existence (64-65).

To overcome this problem, the Rivlin Report suggested that a National Student Loan Bank be established. The bank would be a nonprofit institution established by Congress; it would have power to issue loans to students and to raise capital by floating securities that carried a federal guarantee against default. Students could borrow annually an amount equal to tuition and related fees plus subsistence, minus federal aid received in such forms as National Defense Education Act loans. Loans would be available for five years of undergraduate study and five years of graduate work or the equivalent in parttime study. During the student's enrollment (and up to three years of additional time spent in the Peace Corps, Vista, or military service), the federal government would pay interest to the Bank on all outstanding principal at the average interest rate prevailing at the time the loans were drawn. At the end of the period of enrollment, or enrollment plus service, the Bank would consolidate all of an individual's outstanding loans into a repayment schedule. This schedule might extend for as long as thirty years; it would, however, be a fixed-interest obligation of the borrower, and in the ordinary case no federal subsidy of interest rates would be granted. At the borrower's choice, repayment might provide for a rising schedule, presumably based upon the individual's lifetime income.

This last feature makes the National Student Loan Bank plans appear similar to income-contingent loans, in that repayments are allowed to be small in the early years of family life, when income is relatively low and obligations are growing rapidly. The major difference between the HEW plan and other schemes, however, is that the HEW proposal assumes loans will be paid off in full.

Certain other features of the National Student Loan Bank are similar to those of the Educational Opportunity Bank. First, the student can borrow large sums, sufficient to cover both costs and subsistence; second, the NSLB, as a national, federally sponsored, nonprofit agency, can offer loans of very long term— up to thirty years—which help keep down monthly repayments. Even so, a household with an annual income of $10,000 that incurs $10,000 in loans at an interest rate of six percent (certainly moderate by standards prevailing in the mid-1970s) and repays over the maximum thirty-year period still must contribute 7.3 percent of its monthly income to loan repayment. This is approximately equal to the rate of savings a frugal family of that income level might otherwise achieve. Lower income families would be forced to contribute even larger shares of their income for repayment.

Why do we discuss the NSLB plan in connection with income-contingent loans? In the first place, even though it is basically a fixed-interest plan, some of its features are similar to income-contingent schemes. Also, it includes a more marginal income-contingent feature, a provision that the federal government may cancel annual repayment obligations in cases of unusual hardship. "The provision would provide for cancellation, in whole or in part, of annual repayment in any year in which the borrower's income fails to reach a minimum level and in which the repayment exceeds a maximum percentage of income. Schedules of minimum levels or maximum percentages would be established by the bank in such manner that: (a) in no year does the aggregate cancellation exceed 10 percent of total scheduled repayments to the Bank; and (b) the distribution of cancellations be made to those with the lowest earnings in each age, sex, and family size category" (p. 70).

This provision has a notable strength and an equally notable drawback. The strength is that funds to protect the Bank against losses from low-income borrowers would be drawn from the general reserves of the federal government and not from the earnings of high-income receivers; this would establish an operationally sound basis for the financing of income-contingent schemes, given the strong probability of adverse risk selection. The weakness is that borrowers could never be certain how low their incomes would have to fall before they would be granted relief from a fixed-interest debt. As a result, borrowers would be cautious in undertaking loans. For this reason, the HEW proposal does not seem to promote wealth neutrality toward enrollment in high-cost residential colleges and universities.

We have now considered one privately prepared and two federally sponsored proposals for income-contingent student

loans. Before turning to plans now in operation, we should note
a plan put forward by the state government of Ohio. The Ohio
plan, incorporated in HB 930 of the 1971-1972 regular session
of the General Assembly (though not yet passed) was a package
providing for outright grants up to $510 for students attending
public institutions and up to $1200 for students attending pri-
vate institutions, with grants restricted to students whose parents earned less than $11,000 annually and scaled inversely to
income; an expanded fixed-interest loan plan for students, with
interest set initially at seven percent and funds provided from
the capital of state retirement systems; and finally an income-
contingent subsidy plan, the unique feature of the Ohio approach.

According to the Ohio plan the state had two main objectives in providing an income-contingent subsidy: first, to stabilize tuition fees in public institutions (which had increased at
the state's universities from $350 in 1961 to $720 in 1971);
second, to strengthen private higher education. Subsidiary objectives were to encourage students to make greater use of two-
year community colleges, which are relatively cheap to run,
and, using financial incentives, to encourage students to enter
certain professions where manpower is in critically short supply
—in short, to improve the technological and economic efficiency of Ohio's system of higher education.

Here is the way the plan would work: students attending
public higher education institutions in Ohio would sign a contract pledging that they would pay to the state annually two
percent of their adjusted gross income in excess of $7500 until
the amount of the state subsidies made on their behalf had been
recouped without interest, or until a period of thirty years had
passed after graduation. Payments would be a minimum of $40
a year and a maximum of $2000. Accelerated repayment could
be made. The repayment obligation would apply not to the
total cost of a student's education but only to that amount
which represented a subsidy by the state. Neither unemployed
spouses or the chronically ill would be required to make payments. Out-of-state students would receive a deduction in obligation equal to their tuition fees. Recipients of state grants
would receive a deduction equal to the amount of their grants.

For private institutions, the state would make the following offer: if the institution charged a student fees equivalent to those charged by comparable state institutions, the state would pay the private college or university a subsidy on behalf of that student equal to what the state was making in comparable public institutions. The student would then be obligated to repay the subsidy at two percent of his income in excess of $7500, just as if he or she had attended a public college or university.

No income-based repayment would be required of students who attended community colleges; if they transferred to four-year institutions, however, subsidy obligations would commence. According to the plan, the Ohio state government could offer forgiveness from subsidy repayment to persons who entered critical occupations. As a partial income-contingent loan scheme, this plan has much to recommend it; but since some people would repay nothing and no one would pay back more than was spent on his behalf, without interest, the plan could not be fully self-financing. To be successful, it would require a substantial financial commitment from the state. It would also require cooperation from private institutions to accept students at fees no greater than instructional costs per student in public institutions.

So far we have been considering proposals for income-based loan plans for national or state adoption. Although the concept has not yet been implemented on a large scale, institutional plans are already being used. Two such plans are worth describing—those developed at Yale and Duke.

The Yale Tuition Postponement Option. In 1973-1974, undergraduates at Yale were allowed to borrow up to $1400 a year to meet the costs of tuition fees, room, and board. For each $1000 borrowed, the student pledged to pay Yale 0.4 percent of his or her adjusted gross income for a period not to exceed thirty-five years. A student borrower could opt out earlier in two cases: when he has already contributed 150 percent of his borrowings plus the costs of administering and financing the loan; or when he has paid back at least his principal, and the group of borrowers who began making repayments in the same year has repaid its debt in full at the break-even rate of return, usually one percent above the cost to Yale of borrowing the money to make student loans (naturally, Yale undertakes not to charge students more interest than is permissible under Connecticut loan laws). The plan is intended to be fully self-financing; indeed, a minimum of $29 per year for each $1000 borrowed is charged to students regardless of whether they are earning any income, and over the course of thirty-five years this minimum payment protects the principal of the loan (Johnston, 1972).

An element of subsidy appears in the Yale plan. When Yale enters the money market to obtain funds for student loans, it pledges high-grade securities from its permanent endowment as collateral. The University expects to borrow at near the prime rate. Of course, no student could borrow funds at anywhere near prime rate on a thirty-five-year income-contingent loan. Yale's use of endowment to support students is unusual because none of it is actually used up. At Princeton, another well-endowed institution, a different course is followed, in that some of the capital gains reaped from portfolio management is used to support current operations of the university. Since current operations include financial aid to students, it can be said that both Yale and Princeton use endowment to subsidize student living expenses, although they employ different methods (Rein, 1972).

Tobin (1971) gives the following explanation of Yale's action:

> Throughout the university, admissions applications vastly exceed the number of places available. A business enterprise faced with such dramatic evidence of excess demand for its product would not hesitate to raise its prices. Many students' families can afford to pay more and would willingly, if not cheerfully, do so.
>
> At present tuition they are enjoying a great deal of what economists call "consumers' surplus." But a university is not a business enterprise and cannot charge what it costs to produce its product, let alone what the traffic will bear. Yale is deeply committed to the principle that no one should be excluded because his family cannot afford Yale's charges. We cannot ration Yale education by parental ability to pay.

Here is where the Tuition Postponement Option comes in. Many students whose parents are not affluent would also value Yale education more than it currently costs them. Quite apart from its deeper values, their university education is increasing their lifetime income prospects. But there has been almost no way they can convert any of that future income into cash at the bursar's office today.

Yale administrators do not plan to increase student grants and other nonloan forms of assistance beyond the level prevailing in 1970-1971. This will moderate the rate of advance in mandatory student fees, for part of past fee increases was used to subsidize students, especially low-income students, who would have been squeezed too hard by the increases. About one-quarter of Yale's undergraduate students participated in the income-contingent loan plan in 1971-1972; in 1972-1973 the figure increased to 32 percent.

Under the Yale plan, the negative dowry problem is approached by applying the repayment rate to the income of the participant or to one-half of the joint adjusted gross income of two spouses, whichever is higher. For men at Yale who expect to make a great deal of money, this seems to establish a disincentive to marry women who have borrowed heavily, unless the woman can be counted on to make even more money than her husband.

The Duke Deferred Tuition Plan. At Duke, undergraduates are eligible to defer from $500 to $1000 of fees in exchange for an obligation to pay Duke 0.36 percent of adjusted gross income for each $1000 borrowed for a maximum of thirty years. The opt out point is when repayment reaches principal plus 8 percent interest. Since no one is required to provide a return to Duke in excess of eight percent and since some persons would not yield that much to the university, it is anticipated that Duke will obtain an average return of about five percent. Because the university could make a higher return on other types of investments, there is an element of direct subsidy in the Duke plan (Johnston, 1972).

An unusual feature of the Duke plan is that different

repayment rate structures are established for undergraduates and candidates for various professional degrees—law, medicine, business administration. In general, the terms offered to the candidates for professional degrees are more favorable than are those offered to undergraduates. This practice harks back to the Vickrey proposal that repayment terms should reflect earnings prospects, with relatively lower burdens placed on those likely to earn a great deal. The Duke plan avoids the assessment of each individual's prospects, however, and all that it implies about social class bias, except at the time of screening candidates for admission to professional schools.

Summary

What conclusions may we draw about current efforts to improve the fiscal efficiency of higher education?

Fiscal efficiency requires that the costs of higher education be shifted in some measurable degree from the taxpayer to the private beneficiary. The beneficiary may be regarded as the student's parents, the family in which he or she grew up, or the student himself. Since the legal age of adulthood has been lowered and many students seem to want to become independent of their parents at an early age, it seems reasonable that students will become more responsible for education costs. But the most workable program for shifting costs to students, income-contingent loans, is bound to be regressive in incidence. It can be argued, of course, that financing higher education through taxation is regressive for persons who do not attend colleges and universities at all (Friedman, 1968), a problem we will consider in the next chapter. Yet that inequity does not establish a case for making low-income graduates pay a higher percentage of their earnings into loan schemes than high income graduates.

Though evidence on the point is by no means conclusive, it appears that students from low-income households respond more positively in terms of both college eligibility and college attendance, to offers of low or zero tuition than to offers of high tuition with loans (U.S. Department of Health, Education and Welfare, 1969). Though one might agree with Milton Friedman (1968)—the authors do not—that there are too many persons attending colleges and universities, one may still believe that parental wealth should not determine patterns of eligibility and attendance.

Yet this is the likely result of full-cost pricing combined with income-contingent loans. The financial requirements for low-income youth to attend college are not small. Balderston (1970b, p. 7) states that "students from low income, low education families who now attend college are induced to do so by their own motivations, by the availability of grants and work-study, and to some extent loan financing, and by the availability of income earning opportunity during the summer. . . . Many of them have . . . a strong desire to participate in the lifestyle of middle-class college-going students, at least to the extent of wanting a pattern of life which will involve more or less equivalent cost. And there are good educational reasons why this is often desirable. . . . These are reasons why the cost pattern of attendance is not necessarily low for the student of low income background. They are also reasons why such a student will tend to have a high subjective discount rate." What it comes to, then, is that the low income high school student who realizes that to attend college in middle-class style he must give up five to ten percent of his income over his adult life will decide that it is not worth the effort to establish college eligibility. If this occurs, college enrollment in America could easily continue to display a strong class bias.

Income-contingent loan schemes can be self-financing only as long as college graduates earn substantial incomes and the gap between the average level of income of graduates and nongraduates is maintained. In other words, under these schemes lending authorities, either the federal government or a single institution, would have a stake in increasing the income of college-educated persons. Once the size of its income-based loan holdings became large compared to its total assets, an institution would feel pressured to screen students for their expected income potential even more closely than they do now. Its medical school would welcome a future Manhattan psychiatrist much more eagerly than a future public health physician or researcher.

Under such schemes, students themselves would feel constricted in their career choices unless they were indifferent to the attainment of a certain style of life. Some people might maintain that these pressures, felt both by lending authorities and students, place higher education more clearly in the service of the maximization of GNP, but it is becoming increasingly clear that a high rate of growth in GNP is not a sufficient condition for improvement in the quality of our lives.

Promoting fiscal efficiency, or minimizing taxation to support higher education, by introducing user charges is not a proper goal for higher education. We believe such a step would conflict with the more important objectives of higher education itself, such as achieving a more evenly balanced distribution of enrollment among social classes and improving the measure of choice students have for the uses of their education. Nevertheless, we do not urge irresponsibility in spending funds raised by taxation or in the defining objectives for higher education. Nor do we say that income-contingent loans play no role at all in financing higher education, as we shall see in the next chapter.

4

Providing Opportunities
for All

*E*valuating social efficiency, or
the elimination of the influence of family background on college admissions, is a matter of examining who attends what institutions and how choices about attendance are made. It is generally agreed that certain criteria for admissions to higher education programs are irrelevant—social class, economic status, sex, and race (Green, p. 26). Even so, we still have a long way to go to rid higher education admissions policies of the hateful influence of such factors. Consider black enrollment in colleges and universities. As the Newman task force pointed out (U.S. Department of Health, Education and Welfare, 1971, p. 46) blacks are underrepresented, constituting "only 6.6 percent of college students." The situation of Spanish-surnamed persons is even more appalling. As Sanchez (1971) pointed out in his testimony to the Senate Select Committee on Equal Educational Opportunity, only 1.5 percent of students in the University of California system are Chicanos, even though Chicanos represent 15 percent of California's student population at the secondary level.

The problem is deeper than aggregate measures of enrollment reveal, having roots in public elementary and secondary schools. The Newman report indicates (p. 47) that "another dimension of access is the degree to which minority students are willing, able and encouraged to enroll in all of the different curricula programs of the institution. Black students are concentrated in a few majors, principally in business, education, the social sciences, and the non-M.D. health professions. While lack of adequate preparation in many fields can be compensated for, a weak background in mathematics and science is a recalcitrant barrier to minority students who would otherwise like to major in science and engineering. Unless some improvements can be made in the secondary schools blacks attend, the number of blacks in medicine, science, and engineering will remain low." Similar statements can be made about other minority groups.

The New York State Commission on the Quality, Cost, and Financing of Elementary and Secondary Education (1972, Vol. 1) drew attention to the inadequate educational preparation of minority students from low-income families. The commission noted that New York State has, on the one hand, more high-performing secondary school graduates than any other state; on the other hand, it has the world's largest concentration of recognized educational failures. "The performance of the state's schools is strongly bimodal," the commission notes. "Moreover, . . . the uneven geographic distribution of failure indicates that children in the state's large cities bear the heaviest burden of school failure. And, on the whole, low-income and minority-group students are concentrated in large cities throughout the state." Similar observations are found in Benson and others, 1972. Inadequate preparation of minority students for higher education opportunities is a part of the larger problem of urban deterioration in our country. Women and members of lower socioeconomic groups are similarly disadvantaged in terms of participation in higher education, apart from minority status.

Improved distribution of educational opportunities can be defended in terms of social benefits. First, on a priori grounds, it is impossible to believe that those who are denied access to higher education are without fail persons of lower inherent ability than those who attend. That is, when we find gross underrepresentation of minority groups, are we to conclude that membership in a minority group is equivalent to low aptitude? Logic demands otherwise. A greater representation of minorities, women, and the poor will bring higher education and, later on, the work force, a greater supply of talented people. Second, it is probable that the productivity of our educational system will be increased when the distribution of educational opportunities more accurately reflects the social and racial composition of society. The California State Legislature Joint Committee on the Master Plan for Higher Education (1973, 46-48) points out that "there is a growing body of educational research which indicates that the most selective colleges have the least effects on students. Highly selective institutions make only a slight difference in the student's college achievements (academic and extracurricular), academic ability, likelihood of completing college, level of education achieved and choice of career. . . . In the past, high status has too readily and simply been accorded the institutions which admitted only the 'best qualified' learners. Perhaps in the future the quality of education will be measured in terms of 'value added.' This would look more at the process of education and take into account what happens to the student between entrance and graduation." Perhaps those with this outlook will also be concerned with what happens after graduation. As higher education becomes less selective, institutions will have greater favorable impact on students, and the "value added" by education will increase.

Broadening the distribution of educational opportunities can also be supported under the criterion of fairness, even when persons admitted to higher education who might otherwise be excluded on grounds of race, family background, sex, and so forth, do not possess extraordinary talent. Even in our rich and leisure-filled society, the quality of life is substantially related to how well one uses his talents in the workplace. Guaranteed entry into higher education is an offer of help in developing a person's talents as a worker. This offer is of such fundamental importance to the individual that the availability of higher education should not depend on parental income or background. A number of state courts have said with respect to elementary and secondary schooling that "the quality of education should not be a function of wealth, except of the wealth of the state as a

whole." This statement was made by the California Supreme
Court in an August 31, 1971 ruling on a demurrer in the case
John Anthony Serrano et. al., v. Ivy Baker Priest et. al. Yet we
know that most children of middle- to high-income families
attend college, regardless of whether they possess talent. Justice
demands that equal service be made available to the student of
ordinary ability who lives in a poor household.

Instruction of work skills and nonvocational subjects are
the joint products of higher education. A person who wants to
pursue a serious interest in oriental art and take instruction
from experts may be required to enroll as a fulltime student in a
college or university. In spite of his interest in oriental art, the
person's major department and field of work might be business
administration. Cost considerations force universities and colleges to combine work-related courses and education-as-con-
sumption courses in a joint process of instruction. Likewise,
pursuit of cultural interests may require the individual to justify
such "frivolous endeavors" to himself by saying that they are
incidental to acquiring qualifications for professional work. The
Robbins committee (Great Britain, Committee on Higher Education, 1963, p. 6) quoted Confucius in the Analects that "it
was not easy to find a man who had studied for three years
without aiming at pay. We deceive ourselves if we claim that
more than a small fraction of students in institutions of higher
education would be where they are if there were no significance
for their future careers in what they hear and read; and it is a
mistake to suppose that there is anything discreditable in this."

The criterion of social efficiency may demand that opportunities be made available to poor people of ordinary talent
in order to achieve the goal of income redistribution. Ownership
of physical capital, that is, the material means of production,
such as factories and machines, is now unequally distributed;
further, there is a correlation between the ownership of physical
capital and advanced training, which represents a productive
resource we may call human capital. The ownership of physical
capital and the claim to returns from the investment of human
capital go hand in hand. Higher education can encourage the
acquisition of human capital by those who ordinarily would end
up with little of either income-producing resource.

Defining Criteria

Before we discuss possible means to raise the standard of social efficiency in higher education, we will define the criteria for evaluating it.

Balanced Participation. McConnell has reported that the true proportion of Americans aged eighteen to twenty-one enrolled in higher education in 1971 was about 37 percent (McConnell and others, 1973). Of course, if high school graduates attending proprietary vocational or technical schools were included, this percentage would increase dramatically. What determines college and university attendance? In the first place, a student's academic record, or scholastic ability is an important factor. As McConnell states, "Regardless of socioeconomic background, most of the males in the two higher quartiles of scholastic ability entered some form of postsecondary education." But not all of those top students went on with their studies. In 1967 one-quarter of the high school graduates who scored in the second quartile of academic ability, and who by American standards were plainly qualified for college admission but came from poor families, did not immediately enter any form of higher schooling (Cross, 1971).

Denison (1970) has noted that in the 1965 high school graduating class, 89.3 percent of white males with "A" grades entered a four-year college program while only 46.7 percent of those with "B" grades did. Among white females, 40 percent of those with an "A" average failed to enter any form of higher education. Denison points out that the academic screening process serves to direct economic resources toward the measurably gifted. He estimates that public expenditures in the decade of the 1960s were approximately $5800 a year on white male students who had achieved "A" averages in high school, while the corresponding figures for those with "B" grades was $3200. The resources commitment to white females with "A" grades was $3800, and to those with "B" grades $2500.

Why do some students who rank in the second quartile of ability—the ordinary "B" students—enter college while others do not? And why do many women with superior academic records—"A" students—fail to enroll in any form of higher edu-

cation? A recent study of this matter (Anderson, Bowman, and
Tinto, 1972) suggests that parental background and not, as formerly thought, geographical access to an institution is the domi-
nant factor in the decision to go to college. Speaking of Illinois
youth, the authors report that "among males, the most dramatic effects of parental background occur in the second quarter
for ability. . . . the coefficients ascend steeply and regularly
with education of either parent except for a leveling off when
father's schooling exceeded college completion. . . . Among
girls, the effects of both father's and mother's education appears to be substantial for all ability ranks (but especially for
father's schooling among girls in the lowest category of ability)"
(p. 199).

Obviously, the present system discriminates against poor
students and female students. Does it also withold opportunities
from members of minority groups? The answer depends on how
one looks at the situation. Whereas overall college entrance rates
no longer show any notable degree of discrimination against
minority persons, minority-group students who do attend higher education institutions are found disproportionately in community colleges rather than in four-year institutions. Thus
minority enrollment has expanded mainly in the low-cost sector
of higher education. Paul N. Ylvisaker of Harvard (1973, p. 99)
has noted that "the tendency is to establish a two-tract system:
selective colleges remaining (and perhaps becoming more) elitist, and community and 'newer' colleges short-circuiting their
growing minority and ethnic constituencies into vocational education and careers of less status and earning power."

Moreover, evidence indicates that some students who are
attending community colleges feel that their choices in education have been unduly constrained. "Minority students view
community colleges as second-class institutions, perhaps because they have not had enough access to four-year colleges and
universities and perhaps because of the image of two-year
schools as too vocationally oriented in the old, traditional
sense" (College Entrance Examination Board, 1970, p. 4-3). In
some cases students resent the lack of housing accommodations
or feel that inadequate arrangements are made for transfering

course credits between community colleges and universities. Generally speaking, students are reported to feel that community colleges are underfinanced; compared with the resources students have access to in many four-year institutions, community college students would indeed appear to be shortchanged.

Because admissions procedures in private institutions are likely to remain more selective than procedures in public institutions—within the general category of eligibility, that is—and because students from poor households frequently seem reluctant to borrow heavily for their schooling (as we noted in the last chapter), and because females must be able to act independently of their parents' biases about women's roles and aspirations, the attainment of a balance of social class and sex in enrollment among college eligibles requires a large public sector in higher education that operates essentially on a tuition-free basis. Balderston (1972, p. 12) put the matter this way to the California Legislature Joint Committee on the Master Plan for Higher Education: "The State should meet, to the extent the Federal government does not, the institutional costs of offering public higher education service and that California public higher education should be tuition-free in all types of publicly supported institutions, for all levels of degrees, and for all ages of students." At the same time, high-cost, prestige universities must become more accessible to students from low-income households, to women, and also to students of different ages.

Broadening opportunities to enter higher education with emphasis on overcoming the remaining barriers of poverty, sex, and age should not be defended exclusively in terms of education's role in raising the level of GNP, although historically the apparent contribution of education to the rise in GNP has been impressive. A more inclusive justification for expanding opportunities appeared ten years ago in the report of the Robbins Committee:

> Throughout our report we have assumed as an axiom that courses of higher education should be available for all those who are qualified by ability and attainment to pursue them and who wish to do so . . . we hope there will be little dispute on

the general principle . . . If challenged, however, we
would vindicate it on two grounds. First, conceiv-
ing education as a means, we do not believe that
modern societies can achieve their aims of economic growth and higher cultural standards without making the most of the talents of their citizens
. . . But beyond that, education ministers intimate-
ly to ultimate ends, in developing man's capacity
to understand, to contemplate and to create. And
it is a characteristic of the aspirations of this age to
feel that, where there is capacity to pursue such
activities, then that capacity should be fostered.
The good society desires equality of opportunity
for its citizens to become not merely good pro-
ducers but also good men and women [Great Britain, Committee on Higher Education, 1963, p. 8].

The British government reiterated the same point of view a
decade later in a white paper (Great Britain, Secretary of State
for Education and Science, 1972, p. 34): "Opportunities for
higher education are not . . . to be determined primarily by reference to broad estimates of the country's future need for highly qualified people. . . . The Government considers higher education valuable for its contribution to the personal development
of those who pursue it." In this spirit—viewing higher education
as an end in itself that can promote individual development "to
understand, to contemplate, and to create"—we believe that
college opportunities must be opened to all who are eligible to
attend.

Nondiscriminatory Eligibility. At the present time, primary and secondary school achievement, and therefore college
eligibility, is a function of parental background. Unfortunately,
with information about parents' income, education, and occupation for any large group of young persons, one can make
reasonably accurate predictions of their average academic performance in school. This point is so well documented that no
further discussion is necessary.

What is worth discussing is whether the nexus between
parental circumstances and a child's school achievement can be
broken, and if so, when, by what means, and how quickly.

Programs financed under Title I of the Federal Elementary and Secondary Education Act of 1965, so far the major effort launched in this regard, have had mixed success. Many of the failures can be explained, tentatively at least, by bureaucratic ineptness and obstruction (see Guthrie, 1973, pp. 15-25). We are inclined to take an optimistic view of the value of such efforts, but we believe that removing the deleterious influence of parental background on school achievement is not a direct responsibility of higher educational institutions. The problem must first be attacked in the elementary and secondary schools.

Despite this belief, we recognize that there are some things colleges and universities might do. Because many low-income students perform poorly in school largely for reasons beyond their control, one approach is open admissions, or guaranteed college entrance simply upon evidence of completion of a high school program. This is a good strategy for at least some institutions in a state to adopt, but it is no final solution to the problem of a lower-school failure. Higher education should remain "higher" in its intellectual demands, even though the pattern under which it is structured (fulltime vs. parttime, for example) should be made more flexible and the courses and degrees offered made more varied and appropriate to the interests of the students currently enrolled. If all that is done to meet the problem of school failure is to establish a certain number of open admissions colleges, we can predict that such colleges will be characterized by high drop-out rates and by high-cost remedial programs. Benjamin Rosner of the City University of New York, a pioneer in the open admissions approach, has stated (1970):

> Not even in its wildest moments does the University believe that it will be able to translate every admitted freshman into a graduating senior. In our truly euphoric moments some of us dream about a 50 percent success rate. In our more sober moments we hope for 25 percent. And there are days when 10 to 20 percent looks very good. . . .
>
> Is it worth it? Would the graduation of as few as 20 percent of the 'open admissions student'

population be worth the cost? Do we dare to ask such questions? Unfortunately, we must. The cost of remedial instruction at the university level is from two to four times as great as the cost of remedial instruction at the elementary and secondary school levels, depending upon what factors enter into a determination of remedial costs for students in higher education. Realistically, we cannot expect public funds to continue to provide remedial and other supportive services for students in higher education without looking searchingly at cost-effectiveness ratios. The message for us at CUNY is clear. The University must establish closer working relationships with the public schools in order to attach the problem of remediation where it belongs—at the level of the elementary and secondary school."

If the number of college eligibles among the children of low-income households increased, college attendance in the country would probably rise, for we should not expect middle- and upper-income families to give up the places they expect their own children to occupy. Thus the resource requirements of higher education would grow—but not suddenly. Many potential students prefer to delay the start of their formal higher education until after a period of work or travel, and many enrolled students interrupt their studies with interludes of work and travel. This staggered pattern of college attendance would soften the impact of increasing total enrollments.

Fairness. The fairness criterion we have discussed in previous chapters could lead us to develop stronger objectives for higher education. A stronger set of goals might be to free college attendance from the influences of class; to free student performance from the influences of class (a form of "output equality" in the public sector, this objective is assumed to be attainable if resource commitments are sufficiently massive); to expand the size of all areas of higher education up to but not necessarily beyond the point where returns to higher education measured by the present value of lifetime earnings equal the costs (instruction, books, materials, foregone income) incurred by or on behalf of participants, measuring each employment specialty separately.

We do not deal here with impossibilities. It is not required that every young person attend college, only that each social class be proportionately represented in college attendance in relation to its share of college-age youth. It is not required that all students perform equally well in college, just that each social class have, in terms of currently used ranking schemes, its due proportion of "A" students, "B" students, "C" students, and so on. It is not required that each person earn the same income, for incomes would vary from one occupation to the next, according to the cost of acquiring necessary skills. It is not even necessary that all persons in any line of work make the same amount of money. For example, ability would still be rewarded, as would willingness to work longer or harder. But in any occupation, the average earned income of all workers would bear a definite relationship to the costs of acquiring the skills necessary to enter it.

Would these stronger objectives achieve fairness? Insofar as higher education is a form of consumption that substantially determines a general lifetime pattern of consumption and establishes individual standards of taste, we see no reason why parental circumstances should determine college access for children. Higher education is different from having an expensive watch or taking a trip to the mountains. Presumably, children of richer parents would continue to enjoy more of these pleasures than children of poorer parents—society does not seem to object to differences in the consumption of ordinary items. Yet unlike a trip to the zoo, higher education for many is an intense, sustained experience, continuing over several years of life and allowing an exploration of the human intellect that undirected individual study rarely does. Further, higher education is still the chief determinant of what jobs one is qualified to do—in our society, one cannot practice medicine legitimately without having successfully completed medical school. Fairness demands that talent, initiative, and energy, not the income or education of his parents, determine the kinds of work a person is able to do. If talent in any line of work is inherited, we admit that our argument is flawed, but whether this is so is not at all certain. Energy and initiative may appear to be inherited but more probably are determined by the environment one grows up in. Once we have eliminated the influence of class on college attendance and college performance, fairness would appear to demand that the economic monopoly college graduates hold be removed. Recalling Walsh's argument that one man's income is another man's expense, we should seek to reach the point where returns to education reflect costs. If lawyers receive high fees that cannot be justified by the cost of legal education (which is relatively cheap), then law schools should be expanded and the supply of lawyers increased until the difference between average earnings of lawyers (discounted value) and the average earnings of B.A.'s is equal to the average costs incurred in attending law school. (This is the long-run equilibrium position. If returns do not equal costs at a given time, then the ordinary process of adjustment to an equilibrium position will require that marginal returns and marginal costs be of different size.) We should not continue to extol the virtues of the competitive market, as many of us do, if we are unwilling to see it operate in the supply of human capital.

The result we suggest here would eliminate returns to ability among different occupations, except insofar as the costs of particular forms of higher education are positively correlated with the talents and skills needed to enter different fields. For example, since medical education is an expensive form of higher education, assume that the inborn skills required to be a doctor are higher than those required to become an accountant, for which training is comparatively cheap. Prospective doctors might then see that medical fees, reflecting the expensiveness of medical education, would reward their talent more than would accounting fees. Even recognizing that all rewards for talent would not be eliminated within fields, the fairness criterion suggests that differential returns to inborn skills should diminish over time. Granting that none of us can take credit for inborn talents—or blame for lack of them—this seems a step forward in equity.

Taking into account that the consumption and skill-building outputs of higher education are joint products and that jobs held by highly educated people are often thought to be more "pleasant" than those held by the less educated, it might be thought that if higher education became more widely distributed, educated people would accept rates of pay that failed to return the full costs of their educations. There is, however, one cost of higher education not captured in any current cost measure, the "pain" of acquiring knowledge—serious study is hard work.

Implementing Social Efficiency

We discuss the broader applications of the fairness criterion to show the limits—and we hope, therefore, the practicability—of the reforms we advocate in this chapter. Removing class bias in college and university attendance is the objective we propose for social policy in the field of higher education, even though this goal is only a first step toward the objective of output equality and the more important objective of redistribution of real incomes. Yet even with the limited objectives we propose, problems of fairness arise in choosing the means to implement them. How should a program to remove class bias in attendance among college eligibles be financed?

The major instrument used by state governments to reduce social class bias in enrollment among college eligibles is the public college or university. It is ordinarily heavily subsidized from general revenue sources of the state government and charges students zero or low tuition fees. Assuming that zero tuition is a feasible instrument of policy and that low-income students respond more readily to the offer of zero tuition than that of high tuition combined with loans, we must ask whether zero tuition meets the criterion of fairness. Is it a policy that can, in Rawls's words, be justified to the least advantaged among us? Perhaps surprisingly, this is not an easy question to answer. As we saw in the last chapter, convincing evidence shows that richer families receive more benefits from public expenditures on higher education than do poorer families. This fact does not necessarily settle the matter or indicate clearly that we should charge students and their families more for public higher education, because the rich, even though they make greater use of public universities than do the poor, appear also to contribute to the expenses of those universities in excess of the cost of their use. In short, in public higher education, the rich subsidize the poor under our present policy of low tuition.

How can this apparent contradiction be explained? The easiest way to understand the situation is to examine two tables (*Table 2* and *Table 3*) about a set of hypothetical families. (Hartman, 1970, 519-523. Hartman examines the issues of a long-standing argument between Hansen and Weisbrod on the one hand, and Pechman on the other, over Hansen's and Weisbrod's findings on the costs and benefits of public higher education in California. See also Hansen and Weisbrod, 6(2), pp. 176-191, and Pechman, 5(3), pp. 361-370.) Hartman assumes the existence of a world of nine families, three poor, three middle-income, and three rich, each having one college-age child. The poor families do not participate much in higher education. *Table 2* shows that one student from the poor families is enrolled, attending the type of institution that is cheapest to run ($500). Middle-income families use public institutions thoroughly: all three potential students attend middle-cost institutions such as state colleges ($533). The rich, like the poor, make sparing use of public higher education (two students enrolled) but when they do, they are inclined to go first class, that is, attend the university rather than the community or state college.

The content of *Table 2* has been summarized by Hartman as follows: "All these manipulations are simply another way of describing the raw facts. Poor people pay taxes and very few of them use public higher education. Those who do gain thereby; those who don't, don't. Middle-income people are heavy users of the system. Their taxes don't cover the costs. A few rich people use the system and gain handsomely thereby. The rest of the rich pay substantial taxes and get no direct return." *Table 3* shows net benefits (expenditures made on one's behalf minus taxes paid to support the system) by income class. The primary beneficiary is the middle class. The poor receive a net subsidy,

Table 2

TAXES AND BENEFITS IN PUBLIC HIGHER EDUCATION

Income	$2000				$10,000				$30,000			
Family	A	B	C	Total	R	S	T	Total	X	Y	Z	Total
Students	0	0	1[a]		1[b]	1	1		1[c]	1	0	
Benefit	0	0	500	500	533	533	533	1600	1500	1500	0	3000
Tax	100	100	100	300	400	400	400	1200	1200	1200	1200	3600
Net Benefit	(100)	(100)	400	200	133	133	133	400	300	300	(1200)	(600)

[a] Attends community college
[b] All three attend state college
[c] Both attend public university

Source: From R. W. Hartman, "A Comment on the Pechman-Hansen-Weisbrod Controversy," *The Journal of Human Resources*, V, 4 (© 1970 by Regents of the University of Wisconsin), pp. 519-523.

Table 3
NET BENEFIT BY INCOME

Income	$2,000	$10,000	$30,000
Average Benefit	167	533	1,000
Average Tax	100	400	1,200
Net Benefit	67	133	(200)

Source: Same as *Table 2.*

though smaller than that of the middle class, and the rich suffer a net loss as they should in a progressive public sector.

Our first policy position is that adopting a policy of zero or low tuition fees is one appropriate way of reducing the influence of class on college enrollment. The primary beneficiaries of public subsidy are middle class families, but unless a system for financing higher education has the support of the middle class, it is almost certainly doomed to failure. After nearly a decade of effort to make enrollments in the University of California reflect the social class composition of the state, in spring 1972 36.1 percent of its students came from families having incomes of $18,000 and above, although only 13.8 percent of the families in the state had such incomes (California State Scholarship and Loan Commission, 1972, p. 193). Perhaps the fact that public subsidy of higher education benefits the middle class has not been emphasized because of the resentment against taxes and the pressures applied to university budgets by legislatures and governors alike. Possibly it should be made clearer to middle-class households that as a group they are receiving benefits above the costs they bear in taxes. As long as zero or low fees induce low-income students to attend college, and as long as low-income households receive even a small net subsidy, such tuition policy is appropriate to increasing social efficiency in higher education.

But zero or low fees are certainly not a total solution. Although public higher education has been operating under such policies for a long time, college enrollment is still biased against students from low-income households. Aside from maintaining public institutions that offer zero or low tuition fees, it is apparently necessary to subsidize the living costs of students as well. These costs, as is well known, are not negligible. In 1971-1972, a student from a low-income family (under $6,000) who was attending a community college in California and living with his parents spent an average of $1110 annually to maintain himself (including room and board, books, supplies, transport, clothing, recreation, and incidental expenses, but excluding tuition fees). If he attended a community college and lived alone off-campus, his average maintenance costs rose to $2150. Maintenance costs in the California State University, the University of California, and in private colleges and universities were all proportionately higher.

Table 4 shows average maintenance budgets for students from families with income less than $6000 in the four main sectors of California higher education. The actual budget for any student, of course, would reflect his particular kind of living arrangement (for example, whether he lived at home or not). *Table 4* also shows the proportion of enrollment in each sector of low-income students. As we would expect, this proportion is highest in community colleges and lowest in independent or private colleges.

Students from more affluent homes had higher maintenance budgets while attending college. For example, students from homes in which parental income exceeded $18,000 who attended private colleges and universities had an average maintenance budget of $3660, of which an average of $1840 was contributed by parents (it may also be assumed that in most cases parents paid the fees for tuition). Our immediate interest here, however, is with the student from the low-income home. If he or she is dealt with equitably, and if required public costs are raised by progressive taxation, it is possible to imagine that all students can be dealt with equitably.

According to Table 4, in California (these figures should be reasonably representative of other states as well) a student from a low-income home cannot attend college, even a community college, unless he has at least a parttime job. To attend a

Table 4

SOURCES OF MAINTENANCE BUDGETS
IN CALIFORNIA HIGHER EDUCATION, 1971-1972
(for students from families with less than $6000 income)

Source	Independent College	University of California	State Colleges and Universities	Community Colleges
Parents	$ 340	$ 220	$ 140	$ 130
Employment	950	1180	850	700
Savings	210	140	120	90
Grants and Scholarships	760	670	130	50
Government Benefits	180	230	260	240
Loans	420	390	210	50
Total	$2860	$2830	$1710	$1260

Percentage of Total Enrollment Accounted for by Students from these Families:

	11.2	14.3	18.3	23.2

Note: Does not include tuition fees and related charges. Families with less than $6000 income constitute approximately 32 percent of households in California.

Source: California State Scholarship and Loan Commission, 1972, Appendix 4, Tables 13-16.

state college, a student needs a job even more for he must be able not only to support himself—and in some cases, dependents —but also must have money to pay tuition fees. To attend the University of California or a private college or university, the low-income student requires a parttime job and a grant or scholarship, or a large loan. This situation presents several difficulties. First, it is not easy for young people to get jobs. Many poor youth are at the same time members of minority groups; unemployment rates for minority youth have been as high as 40 percent in such cities as Los Angeles and New York in recent years. Second, the student from the low-income home, often with more than his share of distractions and family responsibilities, is perhaps least served by giving up study time in order to earn maintenance money. Third, consider the case of a poor person who wants to attend an institution of the highest rank. He must first establish eligibility, which is often harder for him than for his counterpart in a wealthier home. But this is only the beginning, for he must also put together a financial package including employment, loans, and grants. The grant is probably the key element, but sizable student grants are still not available in large numbers. For this student, simple eligibility to attend a first-rank institution is not enough. Rather, he must attract a large grant by being outstanding either in scholarship or athletic prowess (especially difficult for female students, rarely considered for athletic scholarships). Since the odds are not favorable for putting together the financial package necessary to attend a university, many young people feel that their efforts to establish eligibility are not worthwhile. On the other hand, simple eligibility is all that is required of the richer young man or woman who almost automatically applies to a college or university.

Our second proposal to raise the level of social efficiency in higher education is for student maintenance grants. Two thousand dollars a year seems to be an appropriate figure for such grants. We believe that grants should not be restricted to persons who grew up in low-income homes, for two reasons. First, making the maintenance grant conditional upon evidence of poverty is demeaning and attaches the stigma of charity to the award. Second, persons of college age, more fervently than they did in the past, want to be independent of their parents. And because many college students are already legal adults, it is appropriate that they be granted their financial independence at age eighteen.

A system of finance of higher education that provided student maintenance grants across the board would, however, unless appropriate countermeasures were taken, have an unfortunate side effect: middle-class and rich families would accept financial assistance in order to make greater use of private colleges and universities. Wealthier students would then push poorer youth out, and private institutions would serve an elite class while public institutions served everybody else. This is certainly to be avoided—there is already too great a class dichotomy between private and public institutions.

Suppose a middle class family had three children approaching college age—or, more correctly, adulthood. They would see that prestigious private institutions charged fees roughly four times as great as the public university, but that the public university nevertheless had respectable academic standing. The family, unless it were educationally very ambitious or the children were unusually gifted, would probably encourage its children to attend the public university. Now suppose the government offered maintenance grants of $2000 a year. Since the family had been expecting to contribute something toward their children's living costs while they were at the university, this amount of money would then be available to apply toward tuition fees at a private university. Taking into account the social status offered by private institutions and perhaps more legitimately the likelihood that the private institutions would be better able to give individual attention to their students, the family would probably now be tempted to have their children apply. If they were turned down, the parents would be keenly disappointed and would probably never be completely satisfied with the public university. If their children were admitted to the private institution, they would likely take places that might otherwise be filled by students from poorer families.

An attractive solution to this problem would be to offer students vouchers for tuition fees, in addition to maintenance grants. In our opinion, such vouchers should be provided by the federal government and be equal in value to two years of fees in a typical private university. For students who chose to attend public institutions, vouchers would cover fees for four full years. To ensure this result, public institutions would be required to regulate fees within the voucher limits. Since the voucher program would actually represent federal underwriting of a major share of instructional costs in public colleges and universities, state governments would willingly cooperate.

How would a poor student find the money to pay fees during the last two years of college if he chose to go to a private institution? Here the income-contingent loan plan described in the preceding chapter has its place, in a role supplementary to maintenance grants and partial assistance toward meeting the level of fees charged in private institutions (students from higher-income families who wanted to be independent of their parents and who were attending private institutions might also wish to borrow from the loan bank). Furthermore, we advocate offering a 50 percent increase in the value of a tuition voucher (but not in the value of maintenance grants) for completion of one year of national service. We admit that the features of this educational finance scheme would be likely to increase competition for places in private colleges and universities—the number of applications to such institutions would probably rise—but as long as the student from a poor home had the financial means to attend, increased competition would not necessarily be bad.

Having come this far, we must now ask whether such generous support of the college student is fair to those who either cannot or will not attend higher educational institutions. The obvious (and we think correct) answer is that it is not. Under the policies we have described so far, those who did not attend college would be forced to help subsidize those who did, while at the same time not receiving any direct benefits. The indirect social benefits obtained by nonattendees, perhaps a justification for their subsidy of others' education, are enjoyed at least as much by college graduates as well.

One way to resolve this difficulty is simply to provide grants to young people without regard to how or where they use the money, whether they pay college fees, travel, buy equipment to start a small business, or put it in a bank to draw interest. Such a policy has actually drawn support from esteemed members of the economics profession. On the basis of an econometric analysis of 1960-1961 data on consumer expenditures of the U. S. Bureau of Labor Statistics, Thurow (1969, p. 329) concludes: "Families desire a substantial amount of lifetime income redistribution over and above that done in 1960-1961, and this redistribution is heavily weighted toward the younger years of a family's life. The actual lifetime pattern of income is a severe constraint on the desired lifetime distribution of consumption expenditures. . . . Lifetime welfare levels might be substantially increased if the constraints on lifetime income redistribution could be lifted. Consequently social planners should investigate methods of eliminating the institutional constraints."

Denison (p. 1202) has stated that "we ought to be thinking of ways to compensate those who do not use public funds for education. As a starter, . . . a payment in cash or government bonds could be considered." Levin (1972b, p. 35) has suggested that "the tacit biases in favor of a narrow form of human capital investment (higher schooling) and in favor of the nonpoor can only be overcome if the government extends its voucher concept to cover a large variety of investments and training. Individuals should be permitted to invest in on-the-job training, apprenticeships, tools, equipment, and ownership of businesses in conjunction with other types of schooling." (A similar, though more tentative, position is taken by Hansen and Weisbrod, 1969, pp. 101-102.) Levin goes on to suggest that the present system hastens the demise of the self-employed person and the small business by encouraging people to acquire knowledge while at the same time making it difficult for them to acquire the complementary physical capital they need to handle their own production tasks.

This kind of proposal has a whimsical quality about it. The idea of cash grants to young people raises images of the money being spent on drugs, of young men and women living idly in communes during the very years when they should be developing their minds, or of a young man taking a quick course in carpentry, buying an expensive set of tools, and then finding that the local powers in the construction trades have no intention of giving him any work.

There are several ways that the voucher plan could be made more realistic. One would be to allow payment of cash only after the grantee had received approval of a youth counselor, perhaps a member of the social welfare corps. The youth counselor would be asked, in effect, whether the particular applicant was likely to make good use of the money he had requested. This solution, however, could become a bureaucratic nightmare. A second approach would be to provide grants for those who did not receive public subsidy for higher education, deferring payment until the age, perhaps twenty-five, when a recipient would be expected to be more responsible in the use of money and more likely to spend it for valid educational purposes. A third approach, the one we shall develop here, would be to confine the subsidy to educational purposes, but to expand considerably the sorts of activities that are defined as education for purposes of subsidy, and to alter radically the conditions under which a person may participate in educational processes.

The first step of such a broadening of eligibility for support would be to make eligibility independent of the applicant's age. Once the plan was put into operation, each person would be entitled to four years of maintenance at a real value of $2000 a year, that is, adjusted to maintain purchasing power against inflation, and education vouchers equivalent to fees for fulltime study for two years in private institutions. If a person chose not to consume these benefits during conventional college years, they would remain available for later use at any time. Further, the grants would not have to be used in one continuous period of study, but could be used to finance a sabbatical year at several different times in a person's life. Some employers might decide, as a part of the fringe benefits offered to their employees, to supplement such federal financing.

The second step would be to specify that persons would be entitled to use their educational grants for a vast range of instructional programs. Any activity in which a person acquired new skills or knowledge would qualify as education, except where either the content (encouraging racial antagonisms, perhaps) or the method (involving physical punishment, perhaps) were antithetical to the social values of the country. Some students could use their grants to acquire high school equivalency certificates. Others might use theirs to study Far Eastern literature and art. Still others could work on acquiring trade skills. The plan might be opposed on the ground that it used tax money to underwrite avocational interests. The rejoinder is that although most undergraduate programs are avocational, nobody

seriously objects to the idea that students receive federal scholarships. Likewise, if objections were raised to using federal money to provide instruction in vocational fields such as carpentry
or barbering, we would point out that while few programs are
more vocationally directed than law school, law students traditionally have been eligible for public support.

We have recommended that students receive substantial
grants for maintenance and fees. Some readers may be curious
about the average size of current student grants. The main programs are those of the federal government. The largest source of
federal funds for student grants is currently the Supplementary
Educational Opportunity Grant program. In 1973-1974, it is
anticipated that $210 million will be distributed under federal
auspices. Average grant per student will be roughly $700, and
larger sums will be available to students in extreme financial
need who would be unable to attend college (or the best college
they are qualified to attend) without an award. However, maximum grants are restricted to an amount no more than one-half
the student's anticipated need and to no more than $4000 for
an undergraduate program or $5000 for a five-year program.

Under the Basic Educational Opportunity Program, it is
anticipated that another $120 million will be distributed by the
federal government. It is estimated that the maximum grant
actually paid (the legal ceiling is $1400 a year) will be about
$450 and the average grant about $250. In short, the expanded
federal involvement in student finance has not yet produced
results dramatically different from the 1971-1972 academic
year, when at the University of California, for example, the
average award from all sources to self-supporting undergraduates was $1010, and only 12.1 percent of students received
awards over $2000.

Aside from the problem that the financial commitment
to student support is still relatively small even from the federal
government, there is the question of whether grants are readily
available to students who attend college at unconventional ages
or who attend in discontinuous intervals. The language of Public
Law 92-318 (Federal Educational Amendments of 1972) does
not seem to bar awards under such circumstances, but the impli-

cation is clearly given in the act that federal grants are ordinarily supplementary to parental support. This is not helpful to the thirty-five-year-old worker who wants to take leave from his job and complete his degree or simply take a few courses in art or music in his spare time.

Proposals for introducing flexibility into the time pattern of education and broadening the definition of education that is eligible for public support have at least two things to recommend them. On the one hand, we cannot expect everyone to pursue studies at the same time or with the same intensity. Older persons may have a keener interest in literature, history, and social sciences than younger people, possibly because they want to apply the knowledge of the real world they have acquired through the experience of living to more abstract or historical disciplines. On the other hand, assuming that it will be some time before we remove the deleterious effects of background on college eligibility, the program we have outlined here allows us to overcome that problem to a considerable degree. Persons who did not perform well in high school could establish college eligibility later by taking a series of tests after having completed a certain amount of home study. Once eligibility was established, they could embark on a college program when it became convenient for them. Further, lack of college eligibility defined in academic terms would not be a bar to participation in many courses or programs with federal support. Public authorities thus would recognize that experience is a reasonable substitute for strictly academic qualifications.

The third step would be to introduce greater flexibility in the academic structure itself. It is entirely possible that the hierarchy of status in higher education, the pyramid whose apex is academic excellence as defined by academics, has become outdated. A different system of organization, with particular reference to California, is described in the following terms by Benson and Benveniste (1972, 202-204):

> A system of higher education that meets the various social functions we discussed would necessarily reapportion resources in a different manner.

It would maintain centers of excellence where those devoted to academic pursuits could continue a traditional form of education. But it would not be a stratified system with opaque barriers where other forms of education are not assumed *a priori* to need fewer resources. It would not be able to expand as rapidly as California's system did because the issue of quantity cannot be divorced from the issue of quality. Our argument is that there is no "cheap" solution to the educational dilemma. The apparent low cost of the junior colleges is only apparent. There has been excessive underinvestment in the expansion of the system of education in California and this underinvestment has had repercussions both inside and outside the system. It leads to and is one of the causes of the malaise that prevails in our societies: the rapid expansion of any system of education which undermines quality leads to widespread dissatisfaction. But this does not mean that "academic" standards are the only ones to apply in the future.

Our utopian model of the university of the future protects quality while recognizing that the university is to fulfill different functions. It is a composite where different program alternatives coexist and where alternatives are provided by special institutions and programs designed to allow transfer or to prepare for transfer.

A form of education that recognizes the various functions we have described is necessarily multipurpose and based on the assumption that motivations that bring students to education differ in content and intensities and these motivations cannot be disregarded. In other words, to the extent some students seek first to obtain credentials, it becomes important to create learning possibilities which make sense to this particular demand. The fact that these students are not motivated (or possibly capable) of the academic interests and excellence which the institutions of higher education value, does not eliminate the existence of potentialities of development in other areas. The missions of the various components of the institutions forming a new model of the university may be different and they can still be linked if they are designed accordingly.

The model for such a university may be a composite of several campuses or administrative jurisdictions—each campus of a size which may not exceed 15,000 students—since there seems to be some recognition that as campus size passes this limit, the flexibility of administration and coordination seems to be lost. But instead of a university composed of various similar campuses (as now constituted) it is possible to conceive of a "geographical" university with campuses in close proximity meeting the different functions now performed by community, state and university campuses. In other words, where the system of education in California is now stratified along levels cutting across the state, it is possible to think of an organic structure based on geographical proximity. For example, the University of California, Berkeley-San Francisco, might be composed of what are at present an array of independent units belonging to the university, the state colleges, and the community colleges in that portion of the State.

Career paths within that structure would allow for faculty service in any of the campuses composing the university. But the campuses would seek to meet different needs and specialize in different areas. Instead of tending toward uniformity across campuses, the policy would be to encourage and create campuses with different objectives. Some campuses might specialize in providing short term employment oriented courses designed to prepare high school leavers for employment at middle levels. Some campuses might specialize in preparing students for transfer from one kind of education to another.

But these diversified campuses with different missions would still provide a single career path for the faculty. Professors might be encouraged through financial incentives to hold appointments in more than one campus and thus achieve an organic integration through participation in more than one program. Moreover, salary schedules, teaching loads, class sizes and other resources would be based on program orientation, teaching and research needs, instead of status level, as is done at present. [See California State Legislature, 1973, for a similar position.]

The last point to note is that if students were encouraged to take advantage of educational opportunities throughout their adult life, and if colleges and universities in any geographical region were organized on the basis of differences in function rather than status, then it would be unlikely and probably undesirable that students would do all their work at any one institution. The assumption that students should seek primary identification with one institution seems to be rooted in two ideas that no longer hold. One idea was that the college was intended to protect students from their own immaturity—to serve, in other words, in the place of parents. Students nowadays prefer to take care of themselves, and as adults they have the right to do so. The other idea was that the college or university needed to have close contact with students over an extended period of time in order to build up a body of loyal alumni who would help maintain the traditions of the institution and give it financial support. But as Lutz has written (1973, p. 21), "None of us who have gone through the new Princeton will make very good alumni."

As an alternative, a student might enroll in a university or college and use it as an academic base. The institution would offer counseling in addition to courses of instruction; it would also have the responsibility to determine when the student had completed the requirements for various degrees. But unlike present practice, the student would be encouraged to take his courses anywhere within the surrounding geographic area in order to obtain the closest possible match between his specialized interests and those of faculty who worked within his field. Not only would this procedure raise the overall quality of instruction available to any student, but it would also help reduce the class considerations that plague colleges and universities.

Summary

To free college eligibility attendance from the influence of social class represents the greatest opportunity to improve the efficiency of higher education within our grasp. Today, unless he is extraordinarily gifted intellectually or physically, a poor youth is unlikely to attend a four-year public institution and highly unlikely to attend a prestigious private institution, plainly a situation that needs correction. Students of similar competence should have the same chance and incentive to go to college regardless of the income or personal assets of their parents, both of which are irrelevant to the decision of going to college or not.

There are two important objectives at stake: moving from a regressive system for distributing educational services, one that favors the privileged classes, toward a fair, progressive system; and shifting the distribution of income from older to younger families.

We propose the following measures to achieve these objectives. First, the practice of charging low or zero tuition fees in public institutions should be continued. Second, all students, regardless of parental income, should be provided maintenance grants of $2000 for four years. Third, all students should be provided tuition grants up to the value of two years' worth of fees in representative private institutions. Fourth, these financial arrangements should be accompanied by a supplementary, national income-contingent loan plan. Fifth, to avoid discrimination against persons who do not choose to attend college immediately after high school or who are not eligible at that time, the financial arrangement should be available at any time during a person's adult life, for discontinuous or parttime attendance. Sixth, a broad range of institutions should be available. The present hierarchical plan should give way to a regional pattern of specialization, to allow a person to study in more than one institution, serially or simultaneously.

5

Looking Ahead

*T*he period of buoyant natural growth in American higher education, sustained by large rises in the numbers of students seeking admission, is drawing to a close. Between 1961 and 1971, the college-age population increased by 44 percent; between 1971 and 1981, it will grow by approximately 11 percent. While the number of eighteen-year-olds—that is, the population of youth at college-entrance age—rose by 39 percent between 1961 and 1971, it will go up by only 2 percent during the decade that began in 1971. The number of high school graduates is forecast to begin declining by 1980. It is inconceivable that the effect of this decline on the college-age population can be offset simply by the fact that a larger proportion of eighteen- to twenty-two-year-olds will seek to attend (National Center for Educational Statistics, 1973, pp. 5-9).

When the college-age population—those from eighteen to twenty-two—was growing rapidly, it was easy for college administrators to defend budgetary increases. For what is easier to explain than the need to build additional structures and hire new faculty to accommodate larger enrollments? And when budgetary increases are easy to defend, concerns about efficiency are quickly forgotten. Higher education expenditures also had political appeal. Governors and state legislators saw that a large and growing number of families had an immediate stake in the expansion of higher education, for the children of those families were or would soon be students. Moreover, the public appeared to believe that institutional research programs would raise our standard of living while helping us solve such problems as urban deterioration and environmental pollution.

Elected officials now find it easier and more politically rewarding to argue for reductions in the public subsidy of higher education in order to hold the line on taxes, than to propose increases. Indeed, it would almost seem politically disastrous for a state official to suggest a tax increase to improve a state's colleges and universities.

Why has this change come about? The answers are without doubt complex and they probably differ from one state to the next. We can, however, make some reasonable guesses.

As we noted, the natural justification for expansion, the rise in the college age population, has slowed down and is heading for decline. Taxpayers find it hard to see why colleges and universities need more money to serve a student population that is not growing.

Expected benefits from research have in some important instances not been achieved. Some new products spawned in university laboratories have turned out to be harmful rather than helpful. The universities have been relatively powerless to alleviate urban decay, racial strife, and environmental deterioration. These failures can easily be translated into a skepticism about the wisdom of spending additional billions on research.

Compared with the early 1960s, the political atmosphere is simply more conservative. Associated with this conservatism is a lingering dislike for the college student tracing back to the student activism during the second half of the 1960s.

Expansion and improvement of postsecondary education is critically important for the quality of life in our country and for the survival of its democratic ideals—otherwise we would not have written this book. Yet, we also believe that in the prevailing climate of skepticism about the future role of higher education, administrators and faculty must, perhaps for the first time, give serious consideration to the four criteria of efficiency. The first four chapters have described the different types of efficiency. In this last chapter, we seek to present a set of practical steps that administrators and faculty members can

take to raise the standards of efficiency in their own colleges
and universities.

Economic Efficiency

Recalling the objective of economic efficiency—fitting
the activities of colleges and universities to those products that
citizens prefer—it is necessary to distinguish between the direct
and indirect actions that administrators and faculty may take.

Neither the administrators or faculty of any single college
or university can by themselves establish a national policy for
human resource development, to ensure a close fit between the
types of advanced training that young people receive and the
jobs they enter. Administrators and faculty can, however, point
out the need for such an objective and offer their time and skills
toward its development, whenever the federal and state governments are ready to act. These educators are in a unique position
to witness and describe the economic and social losses when
young people pursue an arduous course of study only to find
later that society has no use for the knowledge and skills they
have gained. Not only are young people disappointed, but all
those who contributed to their education, including taxpayers,
have suffered a loss.

We discussed various manpower projection techniques in
Chapter One. We also raised the issue of which values should
inform a national manpower policy. The conventional approach
is to rely primarily on guidance from the marketplace. Such an
approach channels young people into lines of work that cater to
families of middle income and above and that appeal to broad
standards of taste—that is, appealing to the mass market that
major advertising accounts seek to exploit. We believe many
administrators and faculty would prefer to see a national manpower policy leavened more positively by humanitarian and
artistic goals. In this country, there are many people who are
poor, crippled, or emotionally lost, even though the human
distress in our own rich country is a tiny share of the world's.
Many young people wish to serve those of us with special needs,
but opportunities for their future employment are still relative-

ly rare. Likewise, great numbers of young people are talented in
the arts: music, writing, dance, drama, painting, and sculpture.
There is a rising number of people who appreciate artistic en-
deavor and would like to see and hear more of it. Yet the
commercial market has not brought these suppliers and consumers of artistic talent together very well. Public policy could
be developed to help do so. If administrators and faculty wish
to see a more humane and artistic set of values guide our policies of human resource development, they should say so.

As for direct measures, those that are within the powers
of administrators and faculty, we suggest, for one thing, that
they obtain guidance from alumni on the proper composition of
courses and methods of instruction in both undergraduate and
graduate education. Obtaining and using such information could
make the content of higher education more closely fit the desired outcome. At the present time, three main groups seem to
determine what is taught and how it is taught in colleges and
universities. One group is faculty within departments. For
example, some departments of English may be inclined to see
that all undergraduates read Chaucer and Shakespeare; other
departments may content themselves with survey courses that
deal with nineteenth and twentieth century literature. The second group is individual faculty members. To a degree, what is
taught and how it is taught in an institution reflects the research
interests of individual faculty members and their predilections
toward particular methods of teaching. The third group is students; they influence the content of the curriculum by their
voluntary enrollment choices.

All wisdom about content of undergraduate and graduate
programs does not rest in the minds of faculty. But students
lack experience to make judgments about program content;
hence, the opinions of students on curriculum, though valuable,
should not be accepted blindly. The opinions of alumni should
not be accepted uncritically either, but they have gained experience in the workplace. They can say what preparation for work
was useful and what was not; further, they know what the
important gaps in their training are. In similar vein, alumni can
offer a perspective on the significance of college education for

their cultural and social lives. Paying heed to alumni opinion
about the relative worth of the different components of higher
education might require hiring faculty with special training; we
would see nothing wrong with this. Furthermore, such a response might help to win alumni support—and even support of
the general public—for the further improvement of higher education.

Technological Efficiency

A high standard of technological efficiency is attained
when resources are used wisely, that is, with a minimum of
waste, to accomplish given ends. Whereas economic efficiency
centers on the relative worth of different end products, technological efficiency is concerned with getting as many desired
products as possible from a given amount of available resources.

No single administration or faculty is likely in the near
future to discover an optimum allocation of resources in higher
education that can be defended on the basis of scientific research. Millions have already been spent trying to discover what
set of instructional activities maximize rates of learning and the
results are at best inconclusive. Thus, the search for new knowledge for a big leap forward in technological efficiency in higher
education is likely to be an indirect activity for most administrators and faculty. They can argue for the need for such new
knowledge and the money to pay for educational productivity
research, but except for a few economists, psychologists, and
educators who are interested in working on the problem, they
will not participate directly.

Increasing technological efficiency in higher education
does not require, however, that we know precisely how many
hours a week a student should spend in classes of what size in
which subjects. There are a number of direct steps, based on
common sense, that administrators and faculty can take. One is
to economize on the use of student and faculty time. Present
arrangements place much greater value on the time of faculty
than that of students. We do not deny that faculty time is more
valuable, and no one would propose that if one faculty member

may lecture to 1500 students, 1500 faculty should attempt to instruct a single student. What should be done is to see what changes can be made to raise the effectiveness in the use of student's time, insofar as it is under the control of the institution, while at the same time avoiding changes that seriously inconvenience faculty.

Faculty have preferences about when they want to hold class. One of the privileges of seniority is to teach in the middle of the morning in the middle of the week. To a degree, departments seek to arrange class hours to minimize conflicts for students, but interdepartmental cooperation is often lacking. The result is that students sometimes cannot take a prerequisite for an advanced course because they must take a conflicting required course in their major. Students often are required to spend more time crisscrossing the campus than makes sense. By examining actual student programs and learning what sequences of courses students would like to pursue if they had no class conflicts, it would be possible to design a campus-wide set of course offerings to reduce conflicts and the time students must spend traveling from one class to the next (the computer, of course, would be a great help in performing this exercise). With such a plan, administrators could see how much disruption the proposed set of course times represented to faculty. Most faculty would probably cooperate if they felt that the burden was being shared—that all faculty were required to give courses at inconvenient times in some semesters or quarters. A similar argument could be developed about the student's need to meet with faculty individually. Some faculty members fail to meet office hours or reschedule them in a manner that is patronizing to—or insulting to the dignity of—students, since students can only assume that the professor places a higher value on his contact with other faculty ("I'm sorry, I can't see you now because I must go to a committee meeting").

Students frequently have to spend a lot of time tracking down books and articles in the library. Heavily used items may be placed on reserve, but the number of reserve copies may be so small as to require the student to check back repeatedly to get what he needs. This procedure can be justified only if stu-

dent time is valued extremely low, for a small diversion in the
college or university budget from faculty salaries to libraries
would allow a significant increase in the availability of the most
commonly used titles. The belittling of the value of student
time reaches a ridiculous extreme when faculty are allowed to
keep library books in their possession for a whole academic
year, preventing students from quick and easy access to these
materials, yet this practice is condoned in some of our major
universities.

Administrators, likewise, can rearrange their own schedules to improve the use of students' time. Students waste hours
in registering for courses, making course changes, obtaining
identification and library cards, petitioning for late exams or
corrections of erroneously reported grades, and so on. Administrators could give the same attention to the "queuing problem,"
subject to the constraints of budget, that efficient retailers do,
and they could shift administrative employees to the desks
where lines are longest, especially at registration time. Almost
any college or university has enough slack in its administrative
staff to allow shifting employees for short periods to give extra
help on registration desks and so on, while suffering little real
loss in the fulfillment of regular assignments.

So far we have been discussing matters that are easy to
think about and, in principle, easy to act upon. There are, however, more fundamental and perplexing matters with respect to
the efficient use of time that should receive serious thought.
Alert administrators should require each faculty member to
examine the content of his courses for clarity, repetition, and
gaps in content. Each department should be required to see if
by shifting a segment of one course to another course, orderli-
ness of presentation could be improved. Each faculty member
should be required to determine whether the learning activities
he supervises represent an efficient use of student time. Administrators should examine the opportunities they have to substitute educational technology, as we noted in Chapter Two, for
the professor. In terms of its use of technology, higher education is one of the last of the cottage industries.

Even more fundamental matters should also be examined.

It is possible that the productivity of some faculty members would be increased if they spent alternating years in full-time teaching and in full-time research (though even when engaged in research they might be working alongside advanced graduate students). Some undergraduates might be stimulated if they were allowed to carry the responsibility for some of the less advanced research activities in their departments. Students might perform better if they interrupted their studies with a year or two in some other activity; administrators might ensure that students could do so. Some students might benefit from being allowed to study on two or more campuses at the same time, and administrators might also ensure that this could easily be arranged.

A second step in raising the standards of technological efficiency is to review the faculty incentive structure. In Chapter Two, we described how administrators might take action to change the incentive structure from one under which faculty encourage students to use up many years of their time in the often fruitless pursuit of the Ph.D. to one under which faculty had interest in seeing their students progress toward degrees. Let us consider another example. Suppose administrators accept the judgment that faculty members are not taking seriously their responsibility for the instruction of lower division students. They might then establish an arrangement under which the final examinations of students in each course—or a random sample thereof—were reviewed by external examiners, that is, faculty from an institution of comparable standing, and the reports of these external examiners were included in the salary and promotion evaluation of a faculty member's work.

Fiscal Efficiency

Fiscal efficiency is attained when the taxes needed to accomplish any social or economic objective are minimized. For example, if wealthy students attending a public university can be induced to pay for a larger share of the costs of their instruction from their own resources, fiscal efficiency is increased. The rationale for this objective is that welfare is maximized when families retain as large a share of their income under their own immediate control as possible and make their own decisions about how to spend it, rather than to have major goods and services, such as higher education, purchased on their behalf by government. This is subject to the condition that an adequate level of social benefits is obtained.

Administrators and faculty who are interested in increasing the level of fiscal efficiency in higher education should support state legislation to raise tuition fees to the level of the full cost of instruction. They should also support legislation under which state governments reimburse parents—or students themselves—for a share of the fees charged by private educational institutions, on grounds that during the period before full-cost pricing in public universities is fully in operation, such subsidy of enrollment in private institutions will reduce the pressure on state budgets. Because full-cost pricing of higher education will unduly discourage attendance by low-income youth, advocates of fiscal efficiency are also well-advised to press for federal and state income-contingent loan plans (Chapter Three).

In addition to supporting legislative change, college and university administrators and faculty can take actions in their own institutions, first by raising tuition fees toward full cost, and second by establishing an income-contingent loan plan for their own campuses, just as Yale and Duke have done (see Chapter Three).

The objective of seeking a higher level of fiscal efficiency in higher education is arguably good and the methods now coming into use—that is, full-cost pricing and income-contingent loan plans—are arguably appropriate for meeting the objective. But we are less convinced of the need for fiscal efficiency than for higher levels of economic and technological efficiency. We see a conflict, moreover, between fiscal and social efficiency (removing the influence of parental background on college attendance and performance). We believe that the combination of full-cost pricing and income-contingent loans is inherently regressive with respect to the distribution of the costs of higher education. It also appears to have regressive effects in the distribution of the services of higher education to different social classes. This package of policies would probably discourage low-income youth from entering college even more than our present system of finance does. Finally, income-contingent credit plans will be solvent only as long as the college-educated receive, on the average, higher salaries than the non-college-educated. If billions of dollars of student credit are at stake in these plans, the country faces a strong disincentive to seriously attack the problem of income redistribution. Therefore, we believe that efforts to heighten fiscal efficiency conflict with the broader goals of higher education. We must recognize also that faculty are increasingly prone to engage in collective bargaining. If such changes in faculty incentives as those we described in the last section are to be obtained, it may be necessary to offer compensation in the form of salary increases. If the brunt of this financial arrangement falls strictly on the fee structure, that is, if the increases in salaries are passed directly fully to students, then the chances that low-income students will be discouraged from attending college becomes even greater and so does the potential conflict between fiscal and social efficiency.

Social Efficiency

Social efficiency in higher education is gained as college attendance and performance become free of the influence of income class, subject to the condition that measures to achieve social efficiency are consistent with the criterion of fairness. This objective represents the greatest opportunity within our grasp to improve the efficiency of higher education. In this country today, unless a poor youth is extraordinarily gifted, he is unlikely to attend a four-year institution and highly unlikely to attend a prestigious university. This is plainly a situation that needs correction, for students of similar competence should have an equal chance and incentive to go to college regardless of parental income or personal assets, both of which are irrelevant to whether one goes to college or not.

There are two important issues at stake: distributing educational services, which now favor the privileged classes, more fairly, and shifting the distribution of income from older to younger families. Any analysis of public sector operations that deals with the question of regressivity and progressivity only in terms of taxes is incomplete; due attention must also be paid to how services are distributed. As we noted in Chapter Four, economic analysis indicates that welfare gains—that is, higher levels of happiness or satisfaction—will be realized when the time pattern of income receipts is shifted toward younger families. We suggest that administrators and faculty support an agenda of legislative and institutional reform to include the following main points. First, the practice of charging low or zero fees in public institutions should be continued. Second, all students, without regard to parental income, should be provided maintenance grants of $2000 for a period of four years. Third, all students should be provided grants for fees in higher education up to the value of two years' worth of fees at the level charged in representative private institutions. Fourth, these financial arrangements should be accompanied by a supplementary national income-contingent loan plan. Fifth, to avoid discrimination against persons who do not choose to attend college immediately after high school or who are not eligible at that time to attend an institution of their choice, the financial arrangement should be available to a person for use at any time during his adult life, and should be available for discontinuous and part-time attendance, as the person desires. Sixth, a broad range of institutions should be available to persons who wish to use their educational grant. The present hierarchical plan among institutions should give way to a regional pattern of specialization by subject and type of instruction, arranged to allow a person to study in more than one institution, even simultaneously. The incremental costs of these recommendations is actually modest—less than 3.5 percent of our annual national product (U.S. Department of Commerce, 1973, Tables 7, 471, 474). Representing income redistribution, this plan favors mainly the young and recognizes, furthermore, that young people enter adulthood at eighteen and desire financial independence at that age.

Broadening the Market

We began this chapter by stating that demographic changes do not favor the continued expansion and improvement of American higher education as long as higher education draws its students mainly from the eighteen- to twenty-two-year-old group. But we have suggested that administrators and faculty may wish to broaden the market for their services by appealing to all age groups. For this to occur, programs in our colleges and universities must become more functional, interesting, and related to the real world than they are now. Demand for vocational courses would probably rise. In the humanities, it would be necessary to find persons who could teach in an open and exciting way, free of condescension and other academic mannerisms. New types of faculty will need to be found and lured into teaching, in some instances on a part-time basis. The educational community, in addition, should encourage employers to offer educational leaves to their workers and to subsidize such leaves at least in part. We believe that the democratization of higher education can be defended on the merits we have demonstrated in this book and that a wider distribution of opportunities for study and reflection over all income and age groups will serve to improve the quality of our lives. Such a transformation of our colleges and universities need not imply that they cannot remain a haven to persons who wish to devote their lives to the explication of the minor works of Xenophon; indeed, it is possible that the chances of preserving such a haven and having it furnished in the style of affluence to which we in academia have become accustomed is strengthened as we become more willing to serve a more heterogeneous clientele.

Bibliography

Adelman, I., and Thorbecke, E. *The Theory and Design of Economic Development.* Baltimore: Johns Hopkins Press, 1966.

Anderson, C. A., Bowman, M. J., and Tinto, V. *Where Colleges Are and Who Attends.* New York: McGraw-Hill, 1972.

Arrow, K. J. "A Utilitarian Approach to the Concept of Equality in Public Expenditures." *Quarterly Journal of Economics,* Aug. 1971, *85* (3).

Arrow, K. J., and Capron, W. M. "Dynamic Shortages and Price Rises: The Engineer-Scientist Case." *Quarterly Journal of Economics,* Nov. 1959, 292-308.

Aussieker, W., and Garbarino, J. W. "Measuring Faculty Unionism: Quality and Quantity." *Industrial Relations,* May 1973, *12* (2).

Balderston, F. E. *The Repayment Period for Loan-Financed College Education.* Berkeley: Ford Foundation Program for Research in University Administration, 1970a.

Balderston, F. E. *Thinking About the Outputs of Higher Education.* Berkeley: Ford Foundation Program for Research in University Administration, 1970b.

Balderston, F. E. "Financing Post-Secondary Education." Testimony given before Joint Committee on the Master Plan for Higher Education. California legislature, Apr. 12, 1972. Mimeographed.

Balderston, F. E., and Radner, R. *Academic Demand for New Ph.D.'s, 1970-90: Its Sensitivity to Alternative Policies.*

Berkeley: Ford Foundation Program for Research in University Administration, 1971.

Balderston, F. E., and Weathersby, G. B. *PPBS in Higher Education Planning and Management: From PPBS to Policy Analysis.* Berkeley: Ford Foundation Program for Research in University Administration, 1972.

Baumol, W. "Macroeconomics of Unbalanced Growth: The Anatomy of Urban Crises." *American Economic Review,* June 1967, p. 57.

Benson, C. S. "Productivity and Collective Bargaining in Higher Education." In *Proceedings of the Twenty-Fifth Anniversary Meeting,* Industrial Relations Research Association, December 28-29, 1972, Champaign, Ill.

Benson, C. S., and Benveniste, G. *Education in California: An Essay on Formal Education in the Post Industrial Era.* Berkeley: University of California Department of Education, 1972.

Benson, C. S., and others. Final Report to the California State Senate Select Committee on School District Finance. Vol. I. Sacramento, 1972.

Blaug, M. *A Cost-Benefit Approach to Educational Planning in Developing Countries.* Washington: International Bank for Reconstruction and Development, 1967.

Blaug, M. "The Correlation Between Education and Earnings: What Does It Signify?" *Higher Education,* 1972, *1* (1), p. 61.

Bowen, H. R., and Douglass, G. K. *Efficiency in Liberal Education.* New York: McGraw-Hill, 1971.

Bowen, W. G. "Assessing the Economic Contribution of Education: An Appraisal of Alternative Approaches." In *Economic Aspects of Higher Education.* Paris: Organization for Economic Cooperation and Development, 1964.

Bowles, S. *Planning Educational Systems for Economic Growth.* Cambridge: Harvard University Press, 1969.

Bowman, M. J. "Education and Manpower Planning Revisited." In *Occupational and Educational Structures of the Labor Force and Levels of Economic Development.* Paris: Organization for Economic Cooperation and Development, 1970.

Breneman, D. W. *An Economic Theory of Ph.D. Production: The Case at Berkeley,* June 1970; *The Ph.D. Production Function: The Case at Berkeley,* December 1970; *The Ph.D. Degree at Berkeley: Interviews, Placement, and Recommendations,* January 1971. Berkeley: Ford Foundation Program for Research in University Administration.

Burns, J. M., and Chiswick, B. R. "Analysis of the Effects of a Graduated Tuition Program at Universities." *Journal of Human Resources,* spring 1970, p. 245.

California State Legislature. Report of the Joint Committee on the Master Plan for Higher Education, John Vasconcellos, Chn. Sacramento, 1973.

California State Scholarship and Loan Commission. *Student Resources Survey.* Report No. 1 of Student Financial Aid Research Series. Sacramento, 1972.

Carlson, D. E. *The Production and Cost Behavior of Higher Education Institutions.* Berkeley: Ford Foundation Program for Research in University Administration, 1972.

Cartter, A. M. "The Supply of and Demand for College Teachers." Prepared for the 125th annual meeting of the American Statistical Association, Philadelphia, Sept. 8-11, 1965.

City University of New York. *Why Free Tuition at City University of New York?* New York, 1972.

Cohn, E. *The Economics of Education.* Washington: Heath, Lexington Books, 1972.

College Entrance Examination Board. *Manual for Financial Aid Officers.* New York, 1970.

Cross, K. P. *Beyond the Open Door: New Students to Higher Education.* San Francisco: Jossey-Bass, 1971.

Daniere, A. *Higher Education in the American Economy.* New York: Random House, 1964.

Deitch, K. "Some Observations on the Allocation of Resources in Higher Education." In S. Harris (Ed.), *Higher Education in the United States.* Cambridge: Harvard University Press, 1960.

Denison, E. F. "An Aspect of Inequality of Opportunity." *Journal of Political Economy,* Sept.-Oct. 1970, 1195-1202.

De Witt, N. "Educational Manpower Planning in the Soviet Union." In G. Z. F. Bereday and J. A. Lauwerys (Eds.), *Educational Planning.* New York: Harcourt Brace Jovanovich, 1967.

Doherty, R. E. "Public Employees Bargaining and Public Benefits." *Labor Law Journal,* Aug. 1971. Reprinted by Educators Negotiating Service, June 1, 1972.

Duryea, E. D., Fisk, R. S., and Assoc., *Faculty Unions and Collective Bargaining.* San Francisco: Jossey-Bass, 1973.

Eberly, D. J. (Ed.) *National Service: A Report of a Conference.* New York: Russell Sage Foundation, 1968.

Frederiksen, N., and Schroder, W. B. *Adjustment to College: A Study of 10,000 Veterans and Non-Veteran Students in 16 American Colleges.* Princeton: Educational Testing Service, 1950.

Friedman, M. "The Higher Schooling in America." *The Public Interest,* Spring 1968, 108-109.

Galbraith, J. K. "Power and the Useful Economist." *American Economic Review,* Mar. 1973, p. 5.

Great Britain, Committee on Higher Education, Lord Robbins, chm. *Higher Education.* London: Her Majesty's Stationery Office, Cmd., 2154, 1963, p. 6.

Great Britain, Secretary of State for Education and Science. *Education: A Framework for Expansion.* London: Her Majesty's Stationery Office, 1972.

Green, T. "The Dismal Future of Equal Educational Opportunity." In T. F. Green (Ed.), *Educational Planning in Perspective.* Guildford, Surrey: Science and Technology Press, 1971.

Guthrie, J. W. "The New Skeptics Have Gone Too Far." In *Conferences on Improving School Effectiveness.* Princeton: Educational Testing Service, 1973.

Hansen, W. L. and Weisbrod, B. A. *Benefits, Costs, and Finance of Public Higher Education.* Chicago: Markham, 1969.

Hansen, W. L., and Weisbrod, B. A. "The Distribution of Costs and Benefits of Public Higher Education: The Case of California." *Journal of Human Resources,* 1969, *4* (2), 176-191.

Harrison, B. "Education and Underemployment in the Urban Ghetto." *American Economic Review,* Dec. 1972, 796-811.

Hartman, R. W. "A Comment on the Pechman-Hansen-Weisbrod Controversy." *Journal of Human Resources*, 1970, *5* (4), 519-523.

Hartman, R. W. *Credit for College: Public Policy for Student Loans.* New York: McGraw-Hill, 1971.

Hettich, W. *Expenditures, Output and Productivity in Canadian University Education.* Ottawa: Economic Council of Canada, 1971.

Hitch, C. J., and McKean, R. N. *The Economics of Defense in the Nuclear Age.* Cambridge: Harvard University Press, 1961.

Hodgkinson, H. "Collective Bargaining for Professors: An Overview." Paper prepared for American Federation of Teachers conference on collective bargaining, Nov. 1973. Mimeographed.

Hoenack, S. "Private Demand for Higher Education in California." Ph.D. dissertation, University of California, Berkeley, 1968.

Hollister, R. *A Technical Evaluation of the First Stage of the Mediterranean Regional Project.* Paris: Organization for Economic Cooperation and Development, 1967.

Howe, R. A. "Bargaining: Evolution, Not Revolution." *College and University Business*, Dec. 1972. Reprinted by Educators Negotiating Service, Feb. 1, 1972.

Jellema, W. W. (Ed.) *Efficient College Management.* San Francisco: Jossey-Bass, 1972.

Jellema, W. W. *From Red to Black? The Financial Status of Private Colleges and Universities.* San Francisco: Jossey-Bass, 1973.

Johnson, H. G. "The Alternatives Before Us." *Journal of Political Economy*, May-June 1972, p. S289.

Johnston, D. B. *New Patterns for College Lending: Income Contingent Loans.* New York: Columbia University Press, 1972.

Judy, R. W. "Simulation and Rational Resource Allocation in Universities." In *Efficiency in Resource Allocation in Education.* Paris: Organization for Economic Cooperation and Development, 1969.

Keller, J. E. *Higher Education Objectives: Measure of Performance and Effectiveness.* Berkeley: Ford Foundation Program for Research in University Administration, 1970.

Kershaw, J. A., and McKean, R. N. *Systems Analysis and Education.* Santa Monica: Rand Corporation, 1959.

Kidd, C. J. "Shifts in Doctorate Output: History and Outlook." *Science,* Feb. 9, 1973, p. 538.

Klinov-Malul, R. "Enrollments in Higher Education as Related to Earnings." *British Journal of Industrial Relations,* Mar. 1971, 82-91.

Ladd, E. C. Jr., and Lipset, S. M. *Professors, Unions and American Higher Education.* Berkeley: Carnegie Commission on Higher Education, 1973.

Layard, R. "Economic Theories of Educational Planning." In M. H. Preston and B. A. Corry (Eds.), *Essays in Honor of Lord Robbins.* London: Weidenfeld and Nicolson, 1972.

Levin, H. M. "The Costs to the Nation of Inadequate Education." Stanford University, Feb. 1972a.

Levin, H. M. "Aspects of Voucher Plan for Higher Education." Occasional paper 72-7, School of Education, Stanford University, July 1972b.

Lutz. C. Statement in *Prospect* (publication of the Concerned Alumni of Princeton), Sept. 10, 1973.

Machlup, F. "Are We Overselling College?" *Princeton Alumni Weekly,* Oct. 12, 1971, p. 6.

McConnell, T. R., Berdahl, R. O., and Fay, M. A. *From Elite to Mass to Universal Higher Education: The British and American Transformation.* Berkeley: Center for Research and Development in Higher Education, 1973.

National Center for Higher Education Management Systems, Western Interstate Conference on Higher Education. *Cost Finding Principles and Procedures.* Boulder, Colo.: Western Interstate Commission for Higher Education, 1971.

National Education Association. *Teacher Supply and Demand in Public Schools, 1971.* Research report 1972-R4.

Nerlove, M. "On Tuition and the Costs of Higher Education: Prolegomena to a Conceptual Framework." *Journal of Political Economy,* May-June 1972, p. S191.

New York State, Commission on the Quality, Cost, and Financing of Elementary and Secondary Education. Report of the commission. Vols. 1 and 3. Albany, 1972.

New York State, Task Force on Financing Higher Education, Francis Keppel, Chm. *Higher Education in New York State.* Albany, 1973.

Nozhko, K., Monoszon, E., Zhanin, V., and Severtsev, V. *Educational Planning in the USSR.* Paris: International Institute for Educational Planning, 1968.

Office of the President, Council of Economic Advisers. *Annual Report.* Washington, D.C.: Government Printing Office, 1971.

Ohio State Legislature. *House Bill No. 930.* 109th General Assembly, Regular Session. 1971-1972.

O'Neill, J. *Resource Use in Higher Education: Trends in Output and Inputs, 1930 to 1967.* Berkeley: Carnegie Commission on Higher Education, 1971.

Organization for Economic Cooperation and Development. *Occupational and Educational Structures of the Labor Force and Levels of Economic Development.* Paris, 1970.

Panel on Educational Innovation, President's Science Advisory Committee. *Educational Opportunity Bank.* Washington: Government Printing Office, 1967.

Parnes, H. S. *Forecasting Educational Needs for Economic and Social Development.* Paris: Organization for Economic Cooperation and Development, 1962.

Pechman, J. A. "The Distributional Effects of Public Higher Education in California." *Journal of Human Resources, 5* (3), 361-370.

Porter, S. "Crises Squeeze on Student Loans," *San Francisco Chronicle,* Aug. 22, 1973.

Psacharopoulos, G. *Returns to Education: An International Comparison.* San Francisco: Jossey-Bass-Elsevier, 1972.

Psacharopoulos, G., and Hinchcliffe, K. "Further Evidence on the Elasticity of Substitution Among Different Types of Educated Labor." *Journal of Political Economy,* July-Aug. 1972, pp. 786-792.

Rado, E. R., and Jolly, A. R. "Projecting the Demand for Educated Manpower: A Case Study." In Mark Blaug (Ed.), *Economics of Education.* Vol. 2. Baltimore: Penguin Books, 1968.

Rawls, J. *A Theory of Justice*. Cambridge: Harvard University Press, 1971.

Rein, R. "Princeton Plays the Money Game." *Princeton Alumni Weekly,* Dec. 5, 1972, 8-11.

Rivlin, A. M. "The Planning, Programming, and Budgeting System in the Department of Health, Education, and Welfare: Some Lessons From Experience." In U.S. Congress Joint Economic Committee, *The Analysis and Evaluation of Public Expenditures: The PPB System.* Vol. 3. Washington: Government Printing Office, 1969.

Romney, L. C. *Faculty Activity Analysis: Overview and Major Issues.* Boulder: Western Interstate Commission for Higher Education, 1971.

Rosner, B. "Open Admissions at the City University of New York." Paper presented at the annual meeting of the American Association for the Advancement of Science, Chicago, Dec. 27, 1970.

Sanchez, D. *Equal Educational Opportunity.* Part 4. Washington: Government Printing Office, 1971.

Schultze, C. L. *The Politics and Economics of Public Spending.* Washington: Brookings Institution, 1968.

Shell, K. "Notes on the Educational Opportunity Bank." *National Tax Journal,* June 1970, 214-215.

Thurow, L. C. "The Optimum Lifetime Distribution of Consumption Expenditures." *American Economic Review,* June 1969, p. 329.

Tobin, J. "Raising the Incomes of the Poor." In Kermit Gordon (Ed.), *Agenda for the Nation.* Washington: Brookings Institution, 1968.

Tobin, J. "The Economics of the Tuition Postponement Option." *Yale Daily News,* Feb. 10, 1971.

Ul Hag, M. "Employment in the 1970's: A New Perspective." In *Education and Development Reconsidered.* Paper prepared for a conference at Bellagio, Italy, May 3-5, 1972, sponsored by the Rockefeller and Ford Foundations. New York, 1972.

United Nations Educational, Scientific, and Cultural Organization. *Access to Higher Education.* Vol. 2. Paris, 1965.

U. S. Congress, Joint Economic Committee. *The Planning, Pro-gramming-Budget System: Progress and Potentials.* 90th Cong., 1st sess. Washington: Government Printing Office, 1967.

U. S. Congress, Joint Economic Committee. *An Analysis and Evaluation of Public Expenditures: The PPB System.* Vol. 3. Washington: Government Printing Office, 1969.

U. S. Congress, Senate Select Committee on Equal Educational Opportunity, W. F. Mondale, chm. *Toward Equal Educational Opportunity.* 92nd Cong., 2nd sess. Washington: Government Printing Office, 1972.

U. S. Department of Commerce. *Statistical Abstract of the United States.* Washington, D.C.: Government Printing Office, 1973.

U. S. Department of Health, Education and Welfare. *Toward a Long-Range Plan for Federal Financial Support for Higher Education: A Report to the President.* Washington: Government Printing Office, 1969.

U. S. Department of Health, Education and Welfare, Office of Education. Report on Higher Education. F. Newman, Chn. Washington: Government Printing Office, 1971.

U. S. Department of Health, Education, and Welfare, Office of Education, National Center for Educational Statistics. Projection of educational statistics to 1980-1981. Washington: Government Printing Office, 1973.

Veblen, T. *The Higher Learning in America.* 1918. Reprinted. New York: Sagamore Press, 1957.

Vickrey, W. "A Proposal for Student Loans." In S. J. Mushkin (Ed.), *Economics of Higher Education.* Washington: Government Printing Office, 1962.

Walsh, J. R. "Capital Concept Applied to Man." *Quarterly Journal of Economics,* Feb. 1935, 469-474.

Walsh, J. R. " '72 Budget: Nixon Proposes Modest Increases for Science." *Science,* Feb. 5, 1971, 459-463.

Weathersby, G. B. *Structural Issues in the Supply and Demand for Scientific Manpower: Implications for National Manpower Policy.* Berkeley: Ford Foundation Program for Research in University Administration, 1972.

Weisbrod, B. A. *External Benefits of Public Education: An Economic Analysis.* Princeton University Industrial Relations Section, 1964.

West, E. G. *Education and the State: A Study in Political Economy.* (2nd ed.) London: Institute of Economic Affairs, 1970.

West, E. G. "Subsidized but Compulsory Consumption Goods: Some Special Welfare Cases." *Kyklos,* 1971, *24.*

Wollctt, D. H. "The Status and Trends of Collective Negotiations for Faculty in Higher Education." *Wisconsin Law Review,* 1971 (1), 18-20.

Ylvisaker, P. N. "Equality and Higher Education." In *Proceedings of the Conferences on Improving School Effectiveness.* Princeton: Educational Testing Service, 1973.

Ziemer, G., Young, M., Tapping, J. *Cost Finding Principles and Procedures.* Boulder: National Center for Higher Education Management Systems, 1971.

Index